Drama free dating is truly a ... ups and downs of finding love in their life. Camie Vincent offers different perspectives from not just herself but many others who have contributed their opinions and words of wisdom. You get to follow along with some characters in the book who demonstrate what a healthy relationship looks like, and what unhealthy love is. Already married myself, I found it helpful to understand my marriage in a fresh light, and also sympathize with the woes and drama I went through while I was dating. Most of all, she helps you to see that being single and dating can be a lot of fun, and true love is definitely worth the wait.
—Alexis Meads, M.A.
　Harvard, Professional Dating Coach

I think there are two things women are afraid of when dating. One is being taken advantage of or abused in some way, and the other is wasting their time with someone who doesn't take them seriously enough. I'm a firm believer that the best way to avoid those pitfalls is to listen to women who have "been there and done that." *Drama Free Dating: Learn From Others, So You Can Stop Wasting Your Time* offers valuable advice from a psychotherapist. Again, as the book title states, the goal here is to "stop wasting your time." The author also uses anecdotes from people of different ages and genders to explain the (sometimes peculiar) differences in how people think about dating and relationships. I would recommend this book to women (and open-minded men) in their twenties and up who are still interested in dating and need some clarity and perspective when navigating the dating world.
—Lynn Gilliard,
　Author of *Let Him Chase You*

The book I wish I would have written. An inspiring empirical look at dating and relationships that makes you dig deep down into the depths of your soul. You find yourself captivated by the character study at the end of each chapter. We have all known these characters throughout our lives and many times can even relate to them on a personal level. The advice throughout the book is subtle but packs a punch. Camie Vincent does a great job utilizing

her education and experience to advise on many different areas of dating that are down to earth and so refreshing. A book I will read over and over and definitely share with as many people and clients as I possibly can. A thought provoking and insightful exploration of dating, love, and relationships that touches the soul. I didn't want it to end.
—Coach T Anthony,
    Author of the book *The Art of Online Seduction*

My honest opinion about the book? I read it in two days! It was a very easy read and extremely relational. I felt that Camie Vincent was able to take every day dating topics and put it into a format that you understood and was also entertaining at the same time. She spoke on things that made me laugh because it was an issue I could totally relate to. That gave me an understanding of what was really going on in most people's lives. I was also surprised about a few topics, such as the online dating information, which was so eye opening, even for an experienced dater like myself! LOL. Overall, I would highly suggest this book for anyone who is in the dating scene or about to enter the dating scene! I am looking forward to having Camie Vincent on my show and introducing her to my listeners. I know there will not be a shortage of topics to discuss!
—Candice Rothenberg
    Host of *Single Parent Show*

Drama Free Dating by Camie L. Vincent is a modernized, practical guide for every man or woman looking for love in today's complex world. Covering the lover's journey from first interaction through to marriage—and with a refreshingly open-minded approach—Vincent strikes a sound balance between romance and reality, research from ordinary folk, and the occasional "hard truth" we all need to hear to take our love life to the next level. Reading this book is a no-brainer if you're seeking deeper and more fulfilling relationships.
—James Melouney,
    Bestselling author of *The Art of Success*

Drama Free Dating

Learn From Others, So You Can
Stop Wasting Your Time

Camie L. Vincent, L.P.C., L.M.H.C.

Drama Free Dating

Copyright © 2017 by Camie L. Vincent, L.P.C., L.M.H.C.

All rights reserved. No part of this book may be reproduced or transmitted in any form or by any means without written permission of the author.

ISBN: 978-0-9993958-0-6 (hardcover)
        978-0-9993958-1-3 (paperback)
        978-0-9993958-2-0 (eBook)

Library of Congress Control Number: 2017959651

Published by:
Pencil To Paper Publishing, Inc.
Duluth, Georgia

This book is dedicated to the first man I ever knew, who will always hold a special place in my heart: my father.

Contents

Introduction..1

1 I Have Been Searching Long and Hard so Where are You?........3
2 Seven Numbers That Mean so Much........................17
3 All in a Simple Click or Swipe............................29
4 The Date Is Set......................................43
5 Keeping Your Eye on the Prize..........................55
6 Two Halves are Better Than One.........................63
7 Be Still My Beating Heart..............................87
8 Active Daters Verses Hoppers...........................99
9 Is it a Bump in the Road or a Boulder?....................109
10 We're Just Friends — Really!..........................129
11 More Than Once in a Lifetime.........................139
12 The Crazy Things We Do for Love......................159

References..171
About the Author......................................175

Introduction

Allow me to introduce myself. I am a single divorced woman that, like so many of us, has been dating for quite some time. I'm a psychotherapist who works with individuals, couples, children, and families. I also write an advice column (blog) on dating/relationships:

www.dearladylove.com.

Long before I became a therapist, people would come to me for dating advice and sometimes, I found myself questioning friends and family about what they thought women or men would do in certain circumstances. I can confidently say that many people hate dating. It's all in the way you look at it, like anything in life. If you think you're going to have a miserable time, you probably will. I've been on more than my fair share of dates. I've learned from these dates and gained volumes of knowledge. I have had some really wonderful dates as well as some truly terrible ones. I met a lot of great guys and never had to walk out on a date. Even if it wasn't going too well, I chose to look for a silver lining. First, it's just one day or night of your life, and second, everyone has something to offer—so although they may not be a potential mate, you may still learn something from them.

People love to listen to my dating stories because many are like something out of a movie, and on some occasions, a slapstick comedy.

I came to the conclusion that a lot of people settle into the first relationship they find. Why? Often because they miss being in a relationship. They are not willing to wait to find someone truly compatible, a person who makes them feel like no one ever has before. Instead, they chose a "Ms. or Mr. Right for Now."

I've been fortunate enough to know some amazing couples who are truly soul mates. You can see it in their eyes and it shows in their actions.

A true romantic at heart, I think when love is in the air, everything seems a little brighter.

I appreciate the opposite sex and often admired men I've met, including wonderful male family members and close male friends (a few are like brothers), and I always enjoyed getting their viewpoint.

Dating can be black and white, but also gray and downright murky. Although women and men are similar, we differ in the way we think.

Both women and men have asked for my advice. At times you wouldn't know the difference between men and women's questions because they are so similar. Other times the questions are so profoundly different it is bewildering.

With all this confusion, one may wish they had a manual to decipher the "secret coded thoughts" running through a potential partner's head.

I wrote this book to explore how people really feel about dating.

In the following chapters, you will get my perspective on dating, some valuable information from various studies conducted over the years, and the uncensored truth from over 100 volunteers I've surveyed throughout the United States. Volunteers ranged from eighteen to eighty-two years of age. They shared their thoughts on many different areas, some pouring their heart and soul into their answers. Some of their names I know, others were anonymous. Does this small group represent how all single people feel about the topics we will be discussing? Definitely not, but they are views of a broad range of people.

I want to make sure I was candid in this book. I love to laugh, and hopefully, you will read something that puts a smile on your face. I didn't want this to come across as a clinical textbook or research study, but I did want to bring my personal and professional experience. We will look into what people want, expect and have done in the name of love, and "get the scoop" on how and why women and men act while dating or in relationships.

Here we go—let's have some fun!

CHAPTER ONE

I Have Been Searching Long and Hard so Where are You?

Here are thirteen little words which will get you started on your journey toward finding love: "What do I want in a partner and where will I find them?"

According to the U.S. Census Bureau, in 2011, 102 million Americans aged 18 or over were single, making up 44% of the population. Fifty-three percent were women, and 47% were men. Sixty-two percent have never been married (a number that has drastically climbed from years ago when people married much earlier), 24% were divorced, and 14% were widowed.

One of my favorite lines from *Sex and the City* sums up this situation perfectly. It was an episode where Charlotte was getting so tired of searching for Mr. Right, and one day she proclaimed to her friends in pure anguish, "I have been dating since I was 15. I'm exhausted! Where is he?!" It is a question so many single people seem to ask (more women than men — sorry ladies).

Where is the best place to meet someone? You can meet people anywhere if you get over the initial awkwardness some people have when talking to strangers.

The first thing you must try to do is be open to meeting new people in a variety of different places, and most importantly, your heart must be open. If you walk around constantly stating that men or women are all "(insert word of your choice here)," then that is what you will attract. Remember there isn't a "perfect" woman or man waiting to make your acquaintance. "Perfect" does not exist.

You might think about giving a chance to someone you've never previously considered dating, and who knows? If it doesn't work out, you may gain a new friend. Sometimes people come into our lives to introduce us to someone else who was meant to cross our path for some other reason. I met one of my closest friends when on a date years ago, while my date and I were at a party. He introduced me to one of his female friends from his hometown, and although it didn't work out with the guy I was with, I gained an incredible friend in return.

Happiness radiates when someone smiles. When you walk by a person who is smiling, you are more inclined to talk to them. So, if you see someone who sparks your interest, flash those pearly whites when you walk on by.

Most people have what we call "a type." It can be a certain look, build or hair color that they seem to be more attracted to than another. They may also have several different "types" that catch their eye. This is especially true with men because they are extremely visual when it comes to picking potential mates. Ladies, whether you want to believe this or not, if a man is not attracted to you in the first 90 seconds (which is how long it takes to form a first impression) he is going to look elsewhere. While women love instant physical attraction, too, a woman is far more likely to become interested after getting to know him even if there is no initial physical attraction. While she may not have been physically attracted the first time they met, over time a woman can be turned on by his intelligence, or his ability to make her laugh. She'll instead feel an attraction to him because of those other factors. Regardless of your sex, being physically attracted to a potential partner is important, but not everything. What's on the inside is the most important criteria to consider.

The way a person makes us feel, the commonalities you share and the way you're able to communicate, is key to forming a solid foundation. Finding someone who resonates with your soul is what's essential. What I mean by the term "resonates" is that you feel a sense of peace, comfort, or at home with this individual.

One way to narrow the "search" is to answer a few important questions.

What are you looking for in a partner? Sit down and make a list of the top qualities, traits, and shared interests you seek in someone you would want to date.

Think about "must-haves" as well as definite "deal-breakers." Take it a step further and think about how you would like your partner to look: brown hair vs. blonde, shaved head, facial hair or not, etc. Think about height: if you're 6'5", do you want to date someone who is five feet tall? What about education? Do you care if they graduated from high school or do you prefer that they have a graduate degree? Is it important that they practice the same religion you do? Do you want kids? Is it okay if your partner has kids? Do you want to live in your current city for many years to come or are you ready to move to another place in a few years? If for example you're sick of the cold and want to eventually end up in Arizona, you may not want to date someone who is committed to your current state until their children are at least eighteen, because Arizona would probably not be an option for them. Would it bother you if your date made less than you? Do you want them to have future goals? Would you prefer an introvert or an extrovert? Do you want someone who is more on the serious side or someone who loves to make you laugh? Do they need to be athletic or love your potbellied pig as much as you do? Write down everything you think of so you can form a mental picture of what you're looking for. For those of you who always hear that you're too picky, you may want to show your list to a friend to make sure it's realistic. There is something to be said about hearing the same thing from others over and over again. There are things we don't want to hear, and we may fight or resist statements, but if different people continue telling you the same thing, you may want to take a long, hard look at what they're saying. Those who care about you want the best for you, remember that.

I don't want you to come up with a rigid checklist, because ultimately, the person you end up with might not be anything like you've imagined. I'm just trying to get you to think about a few "must have's" and definite "deal breakers," so you don't date with blinders on like people have a tendency to do.

Another very practical exercise while looking at what you want in a relationship is to explore what you have been doing. Look at the last three people you have dated and write down everything that initially attracted you to them. Next, review all the reasons why the relationships ended. Look for similarities among the relationships and seek dating patterns you have formed. When you see it in black and white and start circling common themes in your dating history, you'll become more in tune with changes you want to make.

When you first start dating, pay close attention to what they tell you, verbally or non-verbally. In the beginning people are relaxed and really show you who they are. This is the time to look for potential red flags, even though in this stage they can be overlooked because you're excited about this amazing new person.

Carol, one of the women I surveyed, said it's hard to predict who will fall in love, and what people want in a relationship.

"My sister craves someone to take care of her so she never has to work again. I crave trust, honesty, and security. My girlfriend craves a very upbeat, funny, positive man who likes to sail, my other girlfriend craves a man with a big penis who wants sex 4–5 times a week… it's anybody's guess." Loved that answer!

People are searching to find themselves as they look for love along the way.

Very similar, yet, oh, so different.

A notable difference that stands out between the sexes, is men are more comfortable with the way they look than women are. Men don't ask their friends if they think their beer belly (which hangs over their belt) looks bad. There are women who are so obsessed with the way they look from such a young age, that I've had clients in middle school with eating disorders, which is extremely disheartening. The media feeds this frenzy daily, but society is getting better at recognizing that the image of super skinny anorexic women is not healthy. Now, we see more full sized women in undergarment ads, and models have been banned from runways for being too thin since the tragic deaths in 2006/07 of two supermodels. Women scrutinize their bodies far more than any man ever will. Ladies, there are many men out there who won't be concerned with what size your breasts are or if your hips look too large. These men are less concerned about what a woman's body looks like naked; they will just be thrilled you're naked! I recently saw a segment on television about people who are turning themselves into human dolls! It was very scary and sad. These individuals are getting multiple surgeries to look like human Barbie or Ken dolls. That's how far the "perfect image" has been pushed, because we live in a very superficial culture. They focused on two men in the segment as well. Although men usually aren't as concerned about their looks, some do struggle in this area. I previously dated someone who was very concerned about gaining weight.

Another difference in the sexes is that despite social advances, a vast majority of men (starting in their thirties) look for women who are younger than they are, sometimes ranging from fifteen to twenty years or more. The number one thing they are seeking is women that are attractive and sexy, which is again men relying on their visual brains. In some cases, these women are young enough to be their daughter or granddaughter. Men are very competitive by nature and want to show other males what they have acquired, whether it be the dolled up woman on their arm or the membership at the country club. Success has to reach every area of a man's life, as it is vital to a great majority of males. With these couples, if both are happy, that's all that matters because there are complex reasons why they do what they do, and it's not always a Barbie Doll issue. I do believe age is just a number and that there are exceptions to all situations, but overall, with different generations, the gap is too far apart, and it's unlikely to last for the long haul. The main reason couples with a vast age disparity struggle to last is that both parties are usually in it for the wrong reasons. The woman wants to know she is being taken care of and may joke about hoping her partner "slips on a banana peel." The men in these situations are thrilled they have a piece of eye candy on their arm and as one man put it to me plain and simple, "We know it usually won't work." He went on to say, "When we meet one of our buddy's latest young things or worse, if he marries her, we all smirk and bet on just how long it will actually last." Love might not even enter the equation. Instead, the relationships are filled with two people concentrating on getting their needs met. There are couples with a vast age difference who make it work; there are always exceptions. A friend's father was over twenty years older than her mother, and they were happily married until he passed away. On the other hand, I know of one particular couple who is fifteen years apart, and when they were a lot younger, they did everything together and had a lot of fun. When he turned sixty, and she was only forty-five, however, everything changed. He no longer had as much energy as he used to and did not want to do much or go on the wonderful vacations they used to share. The situation only continued to get worse and eventually this woman stated that if she had to do it all over again, she would not have married someone so much older.

Johnny Depp is one of my favorite actors. He and Amber Heard's marriage (a twenty-three-year age difference) which has been labeled "toxic," has come to an unfortunate end. They divorced after being married just fifteen short months.

It can be rainbows and sunshine when you both are young, look and feel great, but as both partners age, both will see and feel the difference. Often, the younger partner ends up taking care of the older partner as they grow older. Overall, women tend to seek out partners closer to their age or older. Some women date younger men (I'm one of them), but predominantly they are not commonly dating men more than a decade younger than they are. Again, there are always exceptions. In September of 2014, psychology researchers at Åbo Akademi University in Turku, Finland surveyed 12,000 local Finns of different ages about their age preference when looking for a mate. They found the majority of the women they queried preferred men of the same age or somewhat older while men preferred women in their mid-twenties. Another interesting fact: the men questioned who were younger than twenty, gravitated toward women who were older, but men older than thirty leaned toward women in their twenties.

Again, there are exceptions, but women struggle with a double-standard. When a woman dates younger, she gets labeled a "cougar" (and this can be even as little as 3–5 years younger), whereas men get high-fives and pats on the back. Some of my male friends complain to me women are "gold diggers" and have even gone so far as to ask them how much they make or what kind of car they drive, because they have a strong desire to be taken care of. Often their long-term goal is finding a man who makes more money than their previous boyfriends or husbands. They want a roof over their head, someone to pay the bills so they don't have to work, and will often sacrifice physical attraction for financial peace of mind. A man wants a woman to show him how much he means to her, and appreciate how much he does for her but doesn't want a woman who is only by his side because of what he may be able to provide. There are also men who aren't bothered by it. When I wrote this, I was living in Florida, where you see both types of situations happening frequently. I'm sure if I lived in a small farm town in the middle of the country, we would not be having the same conversation.

I told my friend recently who is in his forties, that he would be more successful if he chose to stop dating women who were young enough to be his child and quit buying them big-ticket gifts like cars! As it is, he's had a string of girlfriends who loved him and left him — taking their expensive gifts with them. He wasn't having fun!

If we think about it, each and every one of us is looking to get our needs met one way or another, whether it is intellectually, spiritually, sexually, emotionally, or financially. Hopefully more often than not, love is at the top of the list.

I talked to my grandmother the other day; she was reminiscing about the past and shared with me an amusing dating story. I love to hear her stories and as she tells each one of them, I try to envision the time, sights, and sounds of the era. She was living in Savannah, GA during World War II, and the lack of potential suitors was not an issue. Not only because my grandmother was a beautiful woman, but she said the dating ratio was about ten men to every woman (due to all the servicemen stationed there at the time). She went on a few dates with a gentleman, and they had a fantastic time. Showing her just how enamored he was with her, he asked her to marry him and promised to buy her a fur coat if she accepted! As flattered as my grandmother was, she was a strong independent woman and turned down his proposal, holding out for love and not riches. She eventually found love with my grandfather, who she is still happily married to today (and eventually, she got the fur coat).

There are so many ways to meet people and still have fun in the meantime — and the key is having fun! One thing I can say about my life is that I've had a lot of fun. It's what life is all about. You can choose to be happy, see life as an adventure, or be miserable and push yourself to get out of bed and face the world each day. We all have bad days, but the point is, make the good days outweigh the bad. Don't let anyone ruin your day. If you have a conflict in the morning — put it out of your mind by noon. You can choose not to give your day to anyone.

Where art thou?

In 2009 and again in 2010, the internet dating behemoth Match.com hired the research firm Chadwick Martin Bailey to conduct three studies that surveyed over 11,000 participants, to determine where people met their spouses. After questioning 7,000 married couples, the survey found 38% of couples met at school or work, 27% met through family or friends, 17% met online, 8% met at a bar, club or social event, and 4% met at church or a place of worship.

At the end of 2010 (a popular year for dating research), E-Harmony hired Opinion Research Corporation to conduct two studies that evaluated relationship satisfaction. An online survey of 7,386 adults who were married over the past five years (mirroring the sample size and criteria from the Match.com study) were asked how they met their spouse, and then questioned to gauge their relationship satisfaction, using the couples' satisfaction index. Thirty-eight percent met at work or at school, 27% met through family or friends, 12% met online, 9% met at a bar, club, or social event, 9% met somewhere else and 6% met at church or other place of worship. For people fifty and older, online dating was the most popular way they were meeting people, with 27% finding their spouse online. While only 6% met at church or a place of worship, these couples had the highest level of marital satisfaction.

Here is a list I compiled with suggestions on where to find that new "special someone":

Old faithful.
Getting together with family or friends and meeting a girl or guy known by one or all of them in a relaxed atmosphere is a great way to meet someone organically. Or, if they have someone they would love to vouch for and set you up with, it can also be a trusted, safe way to meet someone if you don't mind blind dating. Just don't let Aunt Ida fix you up with your second cousin.

School.
For those of you in college, you're lucky. Talk about an enormous pool of single people! No wonder so many people marry their college sweet hearts!

Social groups.
There are so many different groups you can join for just about any hobby or interest. Meetup.com is a great site for finding new people with similar interests. You name it and there is a group for it, including exercise groups, professional groups, social groups, and so on.

Book stores or coffee shops.
Don't worry, you won't look strange reading a book alone on a Saturday afternoon at your local bookstore, or at your favorite place to get a caffeine fix. Order a cup of java, grab your latest read, and relax. Just don't forget to look up here and there to check out who is coming and going.

The gym.
Healthy people exercising will produce endorphins that put them in a great frame of mind! Plus, the tight work-out outfits can be a definite bonus!

The grocery store.
I once had a guy ask me for my number while I was debating which steak to buy. It is a great place to meet local people who live in your area.

Bars or clubs.
Some people will think I shouldn't put this on the list because they feel there are no "quality" people found in this atmosphere. You just have to be cautious and not give your number to the person at the end of the night who is starting to panic and is anxiously scanning the room for anyone to go home with, because they're afraid of being alone. This is still where a good number of single people go with their friends to unwind, after a long day or week at work.

Church, temple, or other place of worship.
People who have the same beliefs as you do are great connections to make, and many religious organizations have singles groups to help you meet people.

The Internet (dating sites, apps, social networking sites).
Online dating is very flexible. You can correspond with people day or night and communicate whenever you have time. It allows you to be able to meet and get to know a vast majority of potential partners from the comfort of your home, office, or wherever you have access. Potential matches can be sent to your cell phone daily so you never miss an opportunity. You can also put in specific criteria that you're looking for in a woman or man. It's like shopping for a mate! You have to love that!

Charity events.
People from different areas gather at these events, and your money goes to a good cause.

Sporting events like football, baseball, hockey, or whatever your favorite sport is.
Ladies, I know what some of you are thinking: "But I HATE sports!" Consider it this way: literally hundreds of men attend games, because what comes second to sex for so many men, is sports! Also, the beer and greasy food can really hit the spot on occasion.

The pool in your complex or community, or better yet, checking out the pool at a friend's community.
Food for thought: if you date someone in your building or neighborhood, be prepared to see them in the future, even if it doesn't work out. If you feel you don't want to go there, then your friend's pool it is!

Taking a class—whatever your fancy.
Hit the internet or community adult educator and look into that painting, salsa dancing, cooking, or computer class you've been dying to take.

Your neighborhood.
Your local parks, museums, art galleries, library, independent movie theaters and community events like festivals, movies, and concerts under the stars, are great places to meet people!

Work.
I'm not a firm believer in this one, but a lot of people have met this way. Mixing business with pleasure has its pros and cons; it can make the workday much more enjoyable — on the other hand, it feeds the gossip mill and you might lose focus while you're working. The most obvious con is if it doesn't work out, you will have to see them every day or in the future, when perhaps you would rather not.

Playing sports.
Tennis, racquetball, skiing or golf! Practice your favorite sport and look out for the snow bunny in the lodge sitting alone by the fire.

Be one with nature.
Get outside and let the blood flow. Enjoy wherever it is you live. When you're out on your daily walk, jog or run, you will see new people every day, and a few regulars who may peak your interest. Relax on a beach chair while the sounds of ocean waves drown away your stressful work week. Grab a blanket and a picnic basket and sit by a lake, or hike to the top of your favorite mountain; you never know who you may meet on the way up or down.

One man told me he met a woman, who worked as a manager of a company that rents medical equipment. Later that afternoon, he knew she would be leaving something in his mailbox, so he put a large note in it asking her out on a date. It worked — she left him her number. I also know someone who met her husband while stopped at a red light.

A unique story I know is of a couple that met online, but not on an online dating site. They both joined a website where they created avatars in a "virtual world," and were interacting as the people they created in their fantasy world. Eventually they started talking offline and began a long-distance relationship which ultimately lead to marriage.

Chapter Review.

At the end of each chapter, we will be reading about 4 characters (who are purely fictional and to be used as examples of what to do and not to do) who eventually become two couples, as they go through the ins and outs of dating. Here we go:

Meet **Fred**. Fred's longest relationship has been 6 months. He tells the guys he's living the good life because he always has company and doesn't have to spring for dates. He has a lot of girls he calls "friends," some of whom he sleeps with. Lately though, he feels he may be missing out on something, and thinks he may want to "try out" a relationship.

Meet **Myra**. Myra dated someone for a year back in high school, but has not had a long-term relationship since. She is desperately longing for a relationship and can't wait to have a boyfriend again. Myra has been known to call guys every hour "to check in," do their laundry, and once asked a guy to attend a family reunion with her after their first date.

Meet **Bob**. Bob has been in three long term relationships (one lasting five years) and he feels he is ready to settle down, but he just has not met "the right one." He prides himself for being a true gentleman, and feels he knows how to treat a lady.

Meet **Lanie**. Lanie is an expert dater. She married out of high school, but after seven years she and her husband grew in different directions. She would love to marry again, but she will not settle. She started dating again about a year after her divorce and has had a couple of long term relationships since. She hopes to find Mr. Right someday.

Follow these four individuals throughout the chapters and let's see how their stories unfold.

So, to conclude Chapter One, you just never know when, where or how someone is going to come into your life. Always be prepared and be open. If you act like "Eeyore" of Winnie the Pooh and never make eye contact with anyone, you'll have to be careful since you might trip over your own two feet! Your potential sweetheart could be right under your nose, but you must look up long enough to notice!

CHAPTER TWO

Seven Numbers That Mean so Much

Your phone plays a bigger part in your dating life than you probably think. Just how long should you wait before you call? Should you text, call or ping someone on social media? Or why on earth didn't they call or call back? These are all questions that relate to "making contact," which we'll explore in chapter two.

With cell phones storing all our phone numbers, how many numbers do you know by heart? Not a lot, I'm sure. We take the phone for granted, but it is a major tool in communicating while you are dating someone.

I'll describe it as the calling debate: to call or not to call? How long does one wait to call after initially getting a number? Some people are very strict with the two-day rule, and will not pick up the phone to make that call a day sooner, for fear of coming across as desperate. Others will call hours after meeting the person, just to let them know they are on their mind (and to make sure they gave them the right number). Others will hold off to see if the other person calls them instead.

Texting initially made me laugh, because when this wave started sweeping across the nation, I automatically thought a man must have come up with it, and indeed, a man did. Short, sweet, to the point, and they don't get stuck on the phone for extended periods of time. I definitely text and I'm guilty of texting quite often, but I still enjoy hearing a person's voice. Intonation is obviously non-existent in text, so you have to be careful not to read too much into a message as it could be misconstrued. A friend called last month asking me why so many women only wanted to text and not talk on the phone anymore. I said I know a lot of guys who wish they had that problem.

Some people get incredibly upset when they meet a great girl or guy, feel they really hit it off and give them their number, but never receive a call. Don't take it personally. It's not always about you, but we automatically think it is. They could have just got out of a relationship and are not ready to date yet, or they may have met someone else. And what if it was about you? What if they faked hitting it off and weren't that into you, for whatever reason? You know what — it's their loss! It doesn't mean there is anything wrong with you. It's often simply a mismatch or just basic incompatibility. They may not want to get to know you better, but guess what? There is always someone right around the corner that will.

Mystery is obsolete when it comes to the telephone. We know who's on the other end before we pick up. There are no surprises. It seems people are sometimes too connected (posting what they ate for lunch — really?!), and are rarely being seen without the phone attached to their ear or in their hand. However, you can also end up seeing the opposite, which is people only connecting by social media, and rarely using their phones to call. I know a friend who no longer talks to one of her friends, because she was not on the social networking site her friend belonged to. Her friend doesn't use the phone, so she didn't return my friend's calls. If you want to avoid having a relationship that suffers from a less intimate level of human interaction, I suggest not solely communicating with others via social networking. Everyone is busy, but prioritizing who and what matters in your life, and letting people hear your voice once in a while will only strengthen relationships with those you care about. It seems to me some people try too hard to show the world just how "perfect" their life is, when in reality it may be unraveling beneath their feet … People post things that are only truly appropriate for their closest friends to see, not the 500 "friends" on their favorite social networking site. I'm not knocking these sites; they're great for keeping in touch with others. However, I feel a significant number of individuals are over-engaged on their phones at times, to the point where they're not paying attention to what's going on around them as their children or significant other vie for their attention.

Women call men today, but many years ago, that was unheard of. For the most part, even though women can go after whatever they want in life as evidenced by evolutionary psychology—men still prefer to be the hunters, with a prize to be sought after. Try not to cringe after you read that line (either women or men), because I will explain. Ladies: men actually have it in their DNA to go after what they want. They respect what they've worked hard to get, like a job in a top law firm, a boat they always wanted, a promotion they just earned, or the bike they saved up for as a child.

Show him how amazing you are and he will believe it! Show him you don't believe in yourself and he will spot it quick. A man wants a woman with confidence and who takes care of herself. He wants to show her off to the world and if it works out, claim her as his own. (Meaning they're in a relationship, not his piece of property.) When a man really cares for a woman, everyone sees it by the things he does and says. Today, there are some women who make themselves so available they may as well serve themselves up on a silver platter. Just pull the string, and she says "yes, yes," like a bobble-head doll.

The man she met last night texts her at work the next day and she responds in one minute flat. Or, better yet, he gave her his number and she texts him ten minutes after she said goodbye at the sports bar the very same night. Where's the challenge?

He calls at midnight asking her to meet him at a bar for a few drinks, and she is more than happy to oblige. At the end of the night (a Thursday), he asks what she has happening next night, says he thought they could "hang out" at his place, and she smiles and says, "I don't have anything going on. What time do you want me over?" She is silently screaming, "Use me like a favorite childhood toy! I don't have any standards!" More than likely this pair will be going nowhere fast.

Just because people expect things at the snap of their fingers, doesn't mean that is what should be done. Dating is and should be different. Men won't respect a woman he knows he can have without lifting a finger; he won't value her long-term. I'm not saying to act like a primadonna, be difficult and play mind games, I'm saying to have standards and stick to them. Also, this pertains to women who are looking for a relationship.

As for men, women love it when you show you're interested, but please refrain from calling every hour throughout the day and asking her why she needs to hang out with her friends or work so much, etc. It's also not a good choice to call a woman late at night after you've been pounding down a few with the guys, slurring your words and spitting out, "I miss you," after the first date. She will disappear like an ice-cream cone on a hot summer day.

And the survey says…

In the questionnaires my volunteers were given, the men and women had a variety of different answers when I asked about their thoughts, pertaining to when they call, if they call (women), and the inevitable period of waiting for calls.

Do women call men to ask them out on dates?

Well, 50% said they do.

Carol (55) stated, "If he seems interesting, charming, kind, etc. go for it. What do you have to lose?"

Out of the men questioned, 39% reported that they will call a woman who they're interested in right away. Mario (32) stated, "I figure if we enjoyed each other's company, who cares about the rules? Why wait? If I want to talk to her, I'll call."

The second group of men (also 39%) tends to follow the "calling rule." This group stated they will wait one to three days before calling a woman.

In the last group, 22% of the men questioned said they will call whenever it is "convenient" for them, whether it be a day, a week later, or whenever their schedule allows.

What about texting? Do men and women prefer texting instead of talking on the phone?

Well, 70, or 64% out of the 109 people I asked still prefer the phone. The reasoning behind the phone contact for most of them was that it's more personal. You can hear intonation, the nuances in their voice, and the emotion expressed in their words. Twenty-seven people or 25% prefer texting, and twelve people (11%) use both equally, or said it depends on the situation. It also was surprising to me that slightly more women than men preferred texting instead of the phone.

Gabriel (32) said, "It would be easier to text to avoid the awkward, uncomfortable silence between two people who know little of each other, but that is no way to get to know someone. You may as well email her; you'll miss out on the telling vocal pauses and nuances, and the smile in her voice or lack of it. ('Lol' is not an emotion!) Calling is the way to go."

When the volunteers were asked whether they preferred texting or calling, here is what some had to say:

"TEXTING, for sure! I don't like talking on the phone and I don't like the dreaded 'dead air' awkward moments."

"Talking is more personal and human."

"I still enjoy talking on the phone more than texting. Texting is only words, but with talking by phone, you get to listen to the inflection in their voice and it is easier to communicate."

"I prefer to talk to the person on the phone; I like to hear the awkwardness."

"Texting. If I'm not totally comfortable with them it allows me to filter my thoughts and be more careful about what I say."

> "Texting is such a cowardly and yet modern way of contacting, in a very convenient yet lazy way."
>
> "Texting, so I don't have to deal with any awkward moments of silence."

In a 2012 study by the University of Wisconsin, girls took a stressful test then either talked to their mother via telephone, in a face-to-face conversation, IM, or had no contact. Those who communicated with their mothers by instant messaging did not feel they received much comfort at all, similar to those who had no contact. The girls who heard their mother's voice, whether in person or by telephone, exhibited lower levels of stress hormones and an increase in oxytocin, which is a comfort hormone. The power of the human voice calms us much more than any typed word on a screen.

Phones have become a vice for some people, who need to have them either in their hand or close by all the time. I worked with someone who constantly had his phone in his hand or by his side. He had an anxious habit of flipping it around in one hand repeatedly to calm him down.

In April and May of 2011, a study was conducted by Pew Internet Americans Life Project, asking 2,277 adults across the nation by phone who were eighteen years of age and older, whether they preferred calling or texting. Thirty-one percent of people preferred texting, 53% still want to hear an actual voice at the end of the line, and 14% said it depends on the situation. In March 2013, the dating service "It's Just Lunch," reported in a study that they asked 2,901 singles about their dating habits. Seventy-two percent of the people asked were more likely to text someone first after swapping numbers, compared to the 40% who picked up the phone and called. The ironic fact is that 66% admitted to preferring to call, compared to 41% that preferred to text but felt texting was less intimidating. The younger the person, the higher the preference to text. The older the singleton, the higher preference to call. Why did people say they enjoyed texting? Convenience in a very busy world ranked high, but people also said they feared rejection and awkwardness, and felt it was the easiest way to break the ice.

I feel texting has made dating more relaxed. Getting to know one another via text is convenient, but it also takes a lot more time. I've heard some men say getting rejected by text is easier on the ego, which does make a lot of sense.

Female friends and clients tell me how irritating it is when they give a guy their number and all they want to do is text, and not having conversations filled with any substance; there are just quick exchanges here and there. Be upfront and let them know you would like to be called. They may be conditioned to text, but if they want to get to know you better, your phone will ring. Trust me.

Some couples call or text one another every ten minutes of the day in a phone frenzy. Think of it this way. When you start dating someone, if you're not engaged in a chat or text fest as often, the next time you're together, you may discuss something from the day's events that you were unaware of, instead of knowing what they did every minute of the day. Men will text or call more often when you begin dating, then the frequency will decrease. This is natural, so don't be alarmed and think you did something wrong, ladies. They are not your girlfriends and would usually prefer to not have constant chat fests. They go along with it because they care about what makes you happy. Thanks, guys.

Sometimes, instant gratification can be pushed too far. When people call, text, e-mail, instant message you and so on, some people expect an immediate response. If it doesn't happen, they constantly check their phone. Do you find that alarming or normal? Whatever happened to "I will call back when I have a chance"?

Today, I heard a disturbing statistic from a study conducted in 2013 by Nielsen International, who polled 2,021 adults aged eighteen and over on their smartphone usage. One out of ten people, or 9% of people questioned, admitted to being on their phone while having sex! Talk about not being in the moment! Seventy-two percent also reported being less than five feet away from their phone most of the time. Thirty-three percent stated they have been on their phone during a dinner date, which I'm completely against. Unless it is a dire emergency or you are the President, nothing is surely that important. I realize some people are on call 24/7 for their jobs, but I'm fairly certain 33% of Americans aren't that chained to their career and must answer their phone to avoid jeopardizing their job—although I could be wrong. Twelve percent admitted they feel their phone is interfering with their relationship. If this trend of phone use continues, which I'm sure it will, the divorce rate will have another factor to attribute to it. "They paid more attention to their phone than they did to me" will be added to the list of "irreconcilable differences" that lead to divorce. Take that thought to bed at night.

Waiting for the phone to ring.

"Why didn't he call?" or "Why didn't she call back?" The age-old question: Why do people say they will call at the end of a date when they don't intend to? After what you thought was a "great" date, you might have been perplexed by the radio silence. They said, "I'll call you" but didn't. Some say this absently, because they think they're expected to say it even if they have no intention of calling. Not everyone uses it at the end of a date, but unfortunately, a large number do. I think it's better to say, "It was so nice to finally get together, hope you have a great week", "Nice talking to you", or "I had a nice night, thank you" and simply do not discuss anything past the present moment. This way, you don't leave the person with false hope, which is better, but not everyone can pull it off. I think people do prefer to be honest, but feel a little white lie is easier in certain situations. To make this one easy, if they are interested in seeing you again, they'll call. If not, they weren't interested. I know you'd rather believe something extreme happened, but the simplest answer is usually the right one. They just weren't that interested.

There are many reasons a guy or girl may decide not to call, and almost none of them involve being too busy at work or having a sudden death in the family.

The people I questioned said a lack of chemistry was number one for both sexes—a lack of common interests came in second. A top deal breaker for the women was someone who was "rude," and for the men: no "attraction."

One anonymous responder said: "I wouldn't call if the person didn't seem interested in me." When you're on a date and you're interested, show it. There's no need to leave them guessing. Another interesting answer from a handful of people was, if their date did something bizarre, weird or repelling, they wouldn't call again. Let's face it—people are nervous and trying to stand out, but it's never a good idea to be over the top. You want to be remembered for your sincerity, not for your loud comedy act which included sexually inappropriate jokes to the neighboring occupied tables in the coffee shop.

Some of the women said that a deal-breaker was: "If he tried to become sexual too fast."

Male volunteers were asked about how they decide whether to call a woman after a first date. Here's what a few said:

"I call back girls with whom I have a good time, who make me laugh, can keep a nice conversation for a couple of hours, and girls who have a goal in life and are working to achieve it. Anyone else, I would probably not call for a second date."

"Too much personal baggage, too much ex-boyfriend drama, lying (either a big lie or a bunch of little white lies), or if I find out she has kids, because right now they do not have a place in my life."

"I wouldn't call if the date went very bad, meaning that if the person behaved or spoke in strange ways, because the call would probably result in a therapy session."

Female responders were asked how they decide whether to call a man or return his call after a first date. Here's what they had to say:

"If they were rude, obnoxious, needy, or just straight-up weird, I wouldn't call the guy after a date, or likely return his calls."

> "I wouldn't call if I find out they actually have no life and are looking for a life to attach to and are way too clingy sometimes, or if there was just no attraction."
>
> "If they pushed too hard or acted like I was the best thing [ever], I would not call the person back. You want to know that you are equals, not like you are fishing below your means. Also, if there is no connection, I would rather not talk to the person again because I am easily persuaded into a second date, even if I don't want to."

I relate to what one of the men discussed about wanting his dates to have goals, because that's one of my priorities. In the hilarious movie "Think Like a Man" (based on his book), Steve Harvey also talks about how important it is to find out if someone you're interested in has short term as well as long term goals. Like a volunteer also said, men are interested in women that set goals. Goals are not a top priority to everyone, and years ago it used to perplex me, until I realized many people are happy riding the waves and just go with the flow. There is something to be said for that. I find I'm a planner with a lot of goals, but I also like to be spontaneous, go on adventures, and embrace life as it comes.

Men and women have many reasons for not connecting on a first date, but they all end with a silent phone on the other end. Ultimately, the reason you don't hear from a date, is that you just didn't connect. It doesn't mean there is anything necessarily wrong with either of you, it was merely due to a disconnect, as I've mentioned before. There is a good chance you will date more than a few people before you find someone you would like to spend a good portion of time or a lifetime with.

If you run into people who don't call you, just realize this person wasn't for you (what I alluded to on the prior page), go out with your friends, or do something you love.

I feel for men because they undergo a higher amount of rejection than women do. Predominantly, men are still expected to call the woman first, ask her on a date, ask her out again (if he enjoyed himself), and so on. Think about it, ladies—for every man that has ever asked for something as simple as buying you a drink or your number, he had to get up the courage to do so, knowing he may face rejection. Guys, I give you all a lot of credit.

If you are dating someone and it isn't too serious, how often do you expect a call?
Sixty-four percent of men and women surveyed said every two to three days or a few times a week.

The bottom line is, if you are dating someone and say you're going to call, call on the day you say you're going to. In the beginning, you naturally want to make a good impression and stand behind your word. You're not expected to call every day, but try to set the tone by doing what you say you're going to do. Applied here is the phrase: "Actions speak louder than words."

Chapter Review.

Let's follow up on our four characters and see what they're up to.

Fred met a woman in line at his local coffee shop. He asked her for her "Seven digits" and the woman looked at him with hesitation. He went on to say "Come on, I'll show you a good time, baby." The woman turned around and walked away.

Myra and her friend went out after work for happy hour. They met a guy that was there alone, and he and Myra talked and talked because they had a lot in common. When he was leaving, he asked for her number. She gave him her cell and work number, just to make sure he could reach her. He never called and she moped around for a few days, complaining to her friend how upset she was about it.

Bob was out with his brother Saturday afternoon at the local driving range. He looked over to his left, and about ten feet away was

> an attractive girl swinging her club like a baseball bat. He walked over and asked if she wouldn't mind if he gave her a few tips. She graciously accepted, and she and her friend practiced alongside Bob and his brother. Later, they had a drink, and Bob asked Lanie for her number. He called her the next day.

Enough said about telephone etiquette. Oops, I have a call — I better run!

CHAPTER THREE

All in a Simple Click or Swipe

Online dating doesn't have the same stigma attached to it as it did not so long ago. Almost everyone knows someone who met their girlfriend, husband or another online. It's a very convenient way of meeting someone, fitting into even the busiest person's schedule because of the flexible options. Dating apps have become so simplified; you can simply swipe through a parade of photos until someone magically catches your eye. In a study conducted by Pew Research Center in the summer of 2015 with over 2,000 adults, 59% percent of the people surveyed thought online dating was a good way to meet people, versus the 44% back in 2005.

People under twenty-five and those who are in their late fifties to early sixties have the largest growth of dating online. The eighteen to twenty-four-year-old crowd has practically tripled since 2013 (since the last Pew Research Center survey that was conducted on the topic), from 10% in 2013, to 27% in 2015. The growth of this group is due to the use of dating apps. In 2013, only 5% were using them, whereas today one in five reported using them. Six percent of adults who were 55–64 years of age reported using online dating back in 2013, which has now doubled to 12%.

Tools available in the online arena make it easy for you to focus on the type of person you're looking for (as mentioned in chapter one). What age range are you open to? Do you care if they smoke? Want someone who doesn't drink, or drinks quite regularly? Do you care about their political views or what astrological sign they are? Some sites even match you on high levels of compatibility, such as E-harmony and Chemistry.com. This is good because these sites are doing a lot of the legwork for you, saving time it would take organically to find out you may not be compatible or spot something which is a major deal breaker, which traditionally may have taken you a little while to find out. Be cognizant of the fact that people who fill out their profiles and type their answers may or may not be telling you the truth. The show *Catfish* is very popular and there is an overabundance of people who want to be on it. The majority have been strung along, sometimes for many months or years by someone who, for whatever reason, won't agree to meet them. They always have something that has come up, some sort of excuse prepared. Most of the time they've made a fake profile and have been "catfished" by someone pretending to be someone else. Occasionally, there is a success story—two people who are who they said they are, and they ride off into the proverbial sunset. Nev and Maxx are hoping for their first Catfish wedding—and I must say, I don't know them personally, but these two guys seem to be down-to earth, genuine and good people. They are not pretending to care about the people they meet for the ratings, and instantaneously make you feel like they're two guys you'd love to hang out with.

Setting up a Profile.

What should I put in my profile? O.K—think of your profile like a resume for dating. Daters have a lot of profiles to choose from, and you want yours to stand out in a good way.

Let's start with the headline.

You want a catchy headline that isn't like everyone else's. Try to avoid saying something like, "I'm Searching for a Lifetime Partner" or "Looking for a Relationship," these are too common. A few good examples would be something like, "Love Camping, Cuddling by the Fire, Star Gazing, and S'mores!"

or "Wanted: Scuba Partner with a Cute Smile." Make it funny or serious, but make sure your headline is unique.

What a great shot!
Make sure you have a lot of *different* pictures, numbering anywhere from five to ten. This amount isn't too little or too many. Show pictures which best represent you and your personality. Capture images doing things you like to do, such as favorite hobbies and trips you've been on. Make sure the pictures are clear and have a bunch of close-ups, as well as full length pictures. Post pictures that are recent. Recent means no more than one-year old. Two would be the absolute oldest you would want to post. People change each year, so you want to show people accurately what you look like. Make sure your face is clearly visible. Posting every picture with your sunglasses on is not suggested. It's also fine to have a motorcycle helmet or an image of you bundled up in ski gear, because it shows what you like to do. Just make sure the total five pictures shown are not just you skiing in Colorado. If you love photography, wonderful, also a passion of mine—just make sure you're in some of the pictures you take. Men; if you would like to attract a woman who wants you for your money, continue posing in front of your shiny new Ferrari or with your white lab coat with the title, "Dr.____" embroidered on it. Ladies, if you desire men who want you for what's on the outside and not the inside, flaunt that string bikini in every shot, or tell them what a "good time" they'll have with you as you pucker up your glossy lips for the photo. I know I'm being facetious, but you must put out what you want to attract. You choose your target audience. There are a lot of people on dating sites and apps that need someone to review their profiles and ask them honestly what and who they're looking for. If you just want to have fun, that's completely fine, but think about what you're projecting. Some people have spelled out they're just looking for sex in a variety of ways on these sites, and although some won't hold them in high regard, they're at least being upfront and aren't deceiving anyone.

This is me.
In your profile, talk about what makes you different from the rest. Talk about fighting with the bulls in Spain, how you can still do a handstand at fifty, or

your ability to make strangers laugh in any situation. Discuss your likes, personality, and what you're looking for in a partner. Capture yourself in the best light. Let the person get a feel for who you are and what you like to do. You want someone to read your profile and think, "This is someone I'd really love to meet!" Be positive and self-assured. Think of something to catch someone's interest, something people may not know about you. Like how people often notice your Midwestern charm, perhaps you can fix just about anything, or you can mention how one of your secret pleasures is cuddling under the covers on a rainy night watching reruns of your favorite shows, while eating *Reese's Peanut Butter Cups*. I strongly suggest no false advertising. It's never a good idea to say you are years younger or pounds lighter, are a CEO when you're the office clerk, state you have no children when you have five, or put up old pictures from the days you had hair. Yes, maybe you were the hot ticket when the real estate market was strong, used to have a personal trainer and sported rock hard abs, but if that's no longer true, you have to give up on that dream and be a bit more realistic. This doesn't only happen when meeting over the internet. People will feed their dates what they want to hear to get them interested, or because they feel the truth isn't good enough. Be proud of who you are and never let anyone put you down. The only one who can ultimately make you feel inferior about yourself, is you! You shouldn't feel like you need to lie to attract someone. Instead, work on improving the way you feel about yourself. (You are, after all, the most important person in your life.) Value what you have to offer. Even the smallest of white lies is still a lie. My friend went on a date the other night that went very well. The guy she dated went on and on about how happy he was that my friend was so genuine, because he had been on a string of dates where the women had been lying considerably about their weight and/or age. Be honest right from the start—you'll be happy you were if things work out. Speaking of not telling the truth, an April 2015 study by Global Web Index (GWI), on the dating app Tinder proved a lot of the app's users are not single. Sixty-two percent of the users are men, and 38% are women. The study was based on 47,622 Tinder users, aged sixteen to sixty-four across thirty-three countries.

While 54% of the people surveyed said they were single, 30% admitted to being married, and another 12% were in relationships.

Online dating makes hooking up easier and for people who are looking to cheat. It's another way to find new prey or willing participants.

Once you're satisfied with your profile, you're ready to start meeting people. The more effort you put into it, the better the chance is of eventually meeting someone online, as well as in person. In 2005, when Pew Research Center did the first study on online dating, only 43% of people who dated online said they actually went out on a date with someone they met, but when the same study was repeated by them in 2015, the number had increased to 66%, showing that a lot more successful interactions are happening that lead to dates.

Look around.

Take the time to search on sites or dating apps, and read through the profiles you may be interested in. The person may be attractive, which catches your eye initially, but do you have anything in common? A male friend told me that men look at the pictures and maybe read a few lines, but they don't care what you do for a living or what you have to say. They just care that they're attracted to you. As we operate differently, I feel women will take the time to read through the profiles more than men will. Yet, I still believe men who are really looking for an eventual relationship will read what the woman has to say, if they're indeed captivated by the pictures.

Wink or flirt to show someone you're interested.

Send an email to get to know someone. I know some of my male colleagues may disagree, but I advise ladies to show effort, just not too much. Occasional winks and emails are sufficient, and you may contact someone who didn't know you existed because they missed your profile. If you feel like all you're doing is pursuing men, and few are pursuing you, take a break for a bit and reevaluate your profile. If your profile is well written with great pictures, your inbox should be full. I'm not leaning on either side doing less work. I just feel men should do more pursuing, as we went over in Chapter Two, and something you'll also hear in future chapters. Men, I love my life as simplified as possible too, believe me—but instead of sending out the same canned email or I.M. to every one of the ladies you meet, take the extra time and write each one a flattering message intended just for her. Make her feel special, because you paid attention to some of the minor details she put in her profile.

Get to know the person before you decide that they're someone you want to go out with. Ask a lot of questions, as you'll be able to tell a lot from the way they answer. If they continually send curt replies, they're probably just on the site to have a good time. A good tip here is to look at what they wrote in their profile. Can they put together an interesting paragraph? Are they comical? Negative? Did they write something that explains what they're looking for and gives you a snapshot of their personality? Another thing to watch out for—if you're the one that's constantly asking questions and the other person is merely answering and not asking any in return, they aren't putting in the effort to show you they're interested. Think of it like a two-way street. You both should be learning about one another by sending questions back and forth. Some people may hate writing, but if they're really interested in meeting someone, they'll make the effort.

Time to chat.

After you feel that this is a girl or guy you want to meet, exchange numbers and talk to them first. The reason I say this is because through texting, as wonderful as it is, you miss out on a lot. When you hear the person's voice and the conversation flows, it makes you feel better about meeting them and how things may go. Ever talk to someone and the words seem forced, or there are many lulls in the conversation? After the call, you may decide against meeting them after all, and that's OK. If something they've said alarms you, you'll have an answer. If it doesn't sit well with you, don't go because you feel you must. Even if you said you would, you can just as easily say you changed your mind, since you don't owe anyone anything.

If someone asks you out for the upcoming week, but doesn't follow up with a plan and all you hear are crickets, when you hear from them in another week (which you probably will), they're letting you know you're on rotation. Jump off that merry-go-round because you don't have time for games. People send out messages to us time and time again, and a great amount are non-verbal. We just have to read them, and not make excuses or ignore the message, because let's face it, we all want to be wanted. People like to overlook things because it temporarily feels better.

I have a lot to say about this next subject. Unfortunately, it's so common nowadays, it has taken the word "dating" out of many people's vocabularies. It has made things so easy that you find people wonder why they should bother doing anything. Have you guessed it yet? Its sending naked pictures five minutes after you gave them your number. This has become so prevalent and shows someone that not only are you easy to get, but they have nothing to prove in return. It can also show that you feel so bad about yourself, you believe you should try getting someone interested in meeting you by showing them everything right from the start. With men who do this, they just want sex and are going to find the first person who won't get offended by the picture, and hook up as soon as possible. Whether you meet on the net or have been dating for five years, sending naked pictures of yourself is not a smart choice. This is the digital age. The pictures can be sent to anyone, anywhere. The new guy you're talking to can be showing your pictures to all his friends and a few co-workers. Even with someone you're in a relationship with, although you may be in love today, a few years down the line, the circumstances could be different. If you and your girlfriend or boyfriend break up and feelings get hurt, it can turn ugly. They could post those pictures anywhere. It's a big risk and you need to consider if it's worth taking.

Ladies, if you meet a guy you like and you start texting, then after five minutes he says, "Send me a pic," do you think it's a great choice to send him a full frontal? If you want to meet and just have sex, then I guess that would be the answer. But, if you think you like the guy and there might be something between you, then it's a good idea to refrain from sending explicit pictures. What do you think he's going to interpret that as? And, guys, do you really think sending a naked picture to a girl you think is cool is going to make her scream how much she wants you now? Mystery is intriguing for a reason. A few months ago, I talked about this when I was out to grab a drink with a colleague, and he just laughed and proceeded to say, "Watch this." He had been talking and rotating four different girls, all whom he was having sex with. He sent one of them a text and told her to send him a "boob pic." He paused, said, "Wait for it," and in less than two minutes, it arrived in his inbox. I told him what a male whore he was, we laughed and enjoyed the rest of the night.

If you're just looking to hook up, go for it. Just remember, "Netflix and chill" isn't an actual date.

Online dating tips

One: everyone has that one picture where they look amazing. It may be their favorite picture where the lighting is just right, they look relaxed, the color is perfect, and they're proud to show it off. This isn't usually a true representation of what the person looks like. Some sort of attraction is an important component of online dating because all you have initially is the physical attraction as well as what they wrote about themselves. You have no true sense of what they are really like just yet. I suggest you make sure the person has at least three to four pictures in their profile and at least one is a current, clear full body shot. You need to get an idea about what they'll look like in person. I've heard far too many stories about people walking out on, hiding from or being rude to people who didn't look anything like their photos. You want to be pleasantly surprised when they look exactly like or even better than their photos.

Two: don't put your eggs in one basket just yet and don't expect everyone you've been talking to online will continue corresponding with you, just when you think everything has been going great. At any time, they can stop. One downside to online dating is it's like a bunch of kids with ADHD (Attention Deficit Hyperactivity Disorder); it can be hard to stay focused on just one person. Both guys and ladies are talking to many potential partners and may even start getting them confused. It can be overwhelming and because there are so many choices, the one who doesn't meet their needs at the moment for whatever reason, whether it's due to the lack of compatibility, to feeling it would take too long to get them in bed or they can't meet up fast enough, they may end up being ignored. Going into it knowing someone who seems interested in you can drop off anytime is helpful. I hate to have to say this because it seems so negative, but it's true. I'm sure you've heard this from friends if you're just getting back onto the dating scene after many years, or have never dated online. It can happen to anyone. If you go on a date with someone you met via a mobile dating app, online and so on, they may have three other dates lined up that week. It's like gambling. It's a numbers game. Then there's the dater who is so used to dating this way, they're never satisfied and never last with anyone because they're always on the lookout for the next best thing. If you're looking for a relationship and the person you're interested in is over the age of thirty and they have never had a relationship longer than one year-run — this is more likely a time when the saying, "It's not you, it's them," comes into play. They may say they've been unlucky, or their dates are always bad, or act a certain way, and they're really just a nice person; don't believe it. No one is that picky, or has that much bad luck with the opposite sex. With a string of bad dates, the common denominator in those dates is the one bemoaning their fate. It's more likely something in their behavior that has caused this situation to happen.

A study, published in 2014 in the "Cyberpsychology, Behavior and Social Networking" journal claims that people who meet online can result in a greater amount of breakups and less marriages. The data came from a longitudinal study conducted by Stanford University called, "How Couples Meet and Stay Together." They queried 4,002 people across the U.S. who were in relationships or married. During the study, 32% of the couples who were unmarried and had met online had broken up, while 23% of the couples who met in other ways had ended their relationships. They attributed this to the fact that those who meet online may think, "I met this person easily online, and I can just as easily meet someone else." They also felt the respondents who met online seemed like breaking up was less of a big deal because there is such a large pool out there to choose from. Eight percent of the married couples who met online divorced, where only 2% of the people who met offline did. As for marriages: 67% percent of the people who met offline got married, compared to 32% of the couples who met online making it down the aisle. The study concluded that due to the overabundance of options and stigma associated with meeting online (although I think it's not so bad today), daters may take more time before entering a permanent relationship, and it could make them more hesitant in developing a deeper relationship leading to marriage. The woman who wrote the article, Aditi Paul from the University of Michigan said, "If you're looking for love online, try to remember that more choices aren't always a good thing." Through her research and personal experience, she stated, "What I'd encourage is once you find a partner, delete your profile and give it some time." Well said. You want to give the person your full attention and not think about a backup plan (aka other online daters), so you're all in, and not sitting on the fence.

Three: when you meet complete strangers, you must play it safe. Let someone know where you're going on your first few dates until you feel comfortable with them, and meet at a public place. I have heard about too many women who have gone to the apartment or house of someone who they've met online before or after their first date, or invited the person to pick them up for a meet and greet at their place. It's not a good idea. The following stories are extreme and horrific cases. In 2010, a Texas woman gave her address to a man she had been talking to on an online dating site, and we can imagine she was probably excited about their initial encounter. Sadly, the women's two sons found her strangled body when they returned home. In June 2015, another woman met her online date at a bar for their first date, then proceeded to go to his house. He beat her to death and then wrapped her body in a tarp. Both stories are horrific and completely disheartening. Sadly, there were more I could have written about. Before doing the research, I had not heard of anyone who reached their end by the hands of someone they met on the internet, except for the "Craigslist Killer" in 2009. I had heard the story about a woman who was nearly beaten to death by the ex-boyfriend she had met online in 2010, and tried to sue Match.com in 2013 for not advising members on how unsafe internet dating can be, and I was planning to tell you about that story. Conversely, I learned there are roughly 100 murders committed each year by internet predators, which is alarming. There are also thousands of rapes committed (which is my initial concern when people don't heed warnings about showing up at a stranger's home or inviting them to yours), and in a study done in 2005, 25% of rapists admitted they used the internet to find their victims. Now, before you go out and cancel your online membership or forget about ever using a dating app for that matter, remember that these statistics are worldwide, and they are not specific to dating sites/apps. The crimes were committed from individuals who met their victims through various ways on the internet. My intent was not to make you believe all online daters are shady and the world is full of unsavory characters. I still believe there is a higher percentage of good people in this world. There are numerous people who meet safely and successfully online each year. However, it's good to be vigilant and play it safe. Although it may seem like common sense, a portion of these crimes are people who had met someone online and were persuaded into sending these potential love interests/con artists money, gifts, and worse. The victims get pulled into the online con-artist's sob story, and after they have gained their trust over a long period of time, with false promises made of eventually being together, they realize too late they have been deceived.

This goes for men as well. You're not excluded from these statistics. In June 2015, a man arranged to pick up his date at her apartment complex and after he arrived, his date received a phone call. Two men showed up, pointed a gun at him, and demanded all his money. He was shot in the chest and played dead while the three fled the scene. As it turned out, the date was in cahoots with the robbers. He was able to call 911 and got rushed to the hospital. Luckily, he lived to tell his story, but says he is done with internet dating.

I suggest meeting at a public place at least three times or more before letting someone into your home, or going to theirs. The bottom line is, trust your feelings and take these steps only when you feel comfortable. Dating, like everything else, can change. Women should hesitate and consider things, such as if deciding to leave their drink with their date at the bar when they leave to go to the bathroom. A lot is banking on trust and intuition here, if you think about the prevalent fear of the drink being spiked. I'll get into more on "playing it safe while dating" in another chapter.

Four: I suggest meeting people you find on a dating app or online for a cup of coffee for the first date, or another preferred drink. It's kind of like pot luck. You never know what you're going to get. You've developed a connection with a stranger who you've been introduced to through pictures and some appealing lines, and may or may not have heard their voice. You may have formed a mental picture of what they look like and how they will act, but try to stop daydreaming. Although you can hope for the best, you should also be realistic and realize that the vision you've pictured in your mind may only be a little of who they are, and a whole lot of who you imagine them to be.

Hopefully, you're a match and you walk away with a smile and a plan to meet again. If not, you may be disappointed, but just remember, this will happen more while dating online, because when you meet in person, you know you're attracted to the person and had enough in common in your conversations to want to go out on a date with them. Swiping on someone's picture, texting them once the next day, then arranging to meet the next night is not the same. So be brave, keep it light, know you are amazing, and realize there are many ways to meet people, and this is just one other. So, wink, swipe, type, talk, text, and always have hope.

Chapter Review.

Fred went out to eat with a friend one Saturday night and met Laura at the bar. He asked for her number and called a week later. She agreed to go out with him for a drink the following Tuesday. Throughout the date, Fred kept checking out the female bartender and talked about how dreadful the last girl he dated was. He then started talking to the guys a few feet away that were playing pool. The guys asked Fred if he would like to do a shot with them and he replied "Sure!" His date said she needed to go to the ladies' room and never returned.

Myra met a guy on a dating app. They met at a posh new bar that had just opened recently. Myra was early and couldn't wait to see the guy whom she thought would be a perfect match. When he arrived, Myra was attracted to him from the start. She told him how great he looked and how excited she was to meet him. She went on to talk about problems at work, her new puppy, and how she had a hard childhood. Just as her date started to talk about his week, Myra said she forgot to tell him she had a rental because her car was in the shop this week, stating, "Mechanics are such thieves." Shortly after, her date finished his drink, said it was nice to meet her, and left.

Bob called Lanie a few days after their initial conversation and asked her to meet him for Sunday brunch. Lanie wore a new outfit she bought a few days before, and Bob wore a green shirt that matched his eyes perfectly. They met at a quaint restaurant and sat outside. The conversation flowed, they realized they had many common interests, and both listened to one another intently. They had a few laughs and Bob walked Lanie to her car. He hugged her goodbye, said he would love to see her again and that he would call her. Lanie drove away with a smile on her face.

CHAPTER FOUR

The Date Is Set

Aw, the first date. You've been asked out on a date and you're excited. Automatically, you start thinking, "What should I wear?" or "I wonder what they like to do?"

Next, we'll discuss preparations for the date, dating dos and don'ts, where to go, and something you don't want to happen to you—dating disasters!

Set up the date depending when both of you have a few free hours you can block off for some uninterrupted <u>alone</u> time. Dress according to what you'll be doing. Better to dress a bit more subdued than ultra-flashy, so pick out something that makes you look and feel great! Guys, maybe grab a blue shirt to accent those baby blues, and ladies, select something that makes you look and feel like a lady, but still has a bit of sex appeal. Take the extra time to make sure your hair looks great, smell nice, and if you haven't been on a date for a long time, go shopping for a new outfit, or maybe an updated haircut.

Be sure the first date is just the two of you.
Don't bring another couple along for a first date and don't ask if your child can come along. I realize it's hard for some single parents to get a babysitter, but wait a bit longer to schedule the date if you have to, so you have quality alone time before your date meets your children. One way to send a man or woman quickly on their way is to have your bright-eyed child look up at him or her and ask if they are going to be their new daddy or mommy. For those who ask, "Who would do that?" You would be surprised. All the situations I mention in this book I have either heard personally or professionally, except for the hypotheticals I come up with as comedic examples.

Avoid discussing anything too heavy on your first date.
Keep topics light and upbeat. Say something that may make your date smile. And don't forget everyone loves a good compliment.

It's not okay to talk about your ex and what an awful person they were while using some lovely adjectives to describe them. When you're acting angry and bitter, it shows you're not in control of your emotions. It will also make the other person think, "Hmm, if I ever got into a relationship with this person and we broke up, what would they be telling their future dates about me? Better yet, how do they handle adversity?" For those of you who are going through any kind of life crisis, your date does not need to know. Well, not initially.

I'm not saying you should appear as a Pollyanna. Just wait a while to spill the beans.

Deal with whatever issues you have, and be emotionally available and stable before you jump back into the dating scene.
You will feel so much healthier and your future relationships will have a greater chance of succeeding if you're emotionally available. Otherwise, take the extra time to heal. Be patient with yourself.

Try to keep a positive state of mind and get to know the other person.
Walk toward your date with the intention that it's going to be a great date! Discuss stories that put you in the best light. People like to talk about themselves,

so ask questions, look them in the eyes, and listen. Paul Tillich, a German philosopher, was quoted as saying, "The first duty of love is to listen." If you're looking for love, this is an essential tool to have in your toolbox, and it'll surely be worth its weight in gold once it's mastered.

My friend went out with someone who stared at the TV the entire time and wouldn't make eye contact with her. She walked away saying, "I guess there must have been a game that was more important!" Act like what the person is telling you is the most interesting thing you've heard in a while. We were only given one mouth, but two ears.

Learn all you can about the other person.
You want to look at a person's lifestyle, evaluate the way they treat others, and find out what makes them tick. Compare your commonalities. Since opposites attract, a partner who has a very different personality than you can be quite refreshing, so you can learn from one another. Just make sure you have enough of a common ground to keep things interesting. On the other hand, when you get two people who have a lot in common, all their similarities can make them tighter than Siamese twins. Either way, the glue that usually makes couples stick is being on the same page quite often. There can be diversity and differences, but there must be similarities when looking at key areas. These are areas such as shared interests, goals, time spent together, work ethic, philosophies on life, income level, education, level of support and compromise, external relationships (family/friends), and other shared values. Being able to communicate well and "enjoy" talking to one another in a relaxed, comfortable and open manner is essential to any relationship. Pay close attention to the way your date treats you. If a woman is very attractive but talks about herself during the entire date, she probably isn't the woman that will be as interested in you as you are in her. Try to avoid getting fixated on the way a woman looks because looks fade, but someone's personality will not change. Search for the person who you can't wait to tell all about your day, someone that will listen with interest.

Talk about hobbies, what interests you, sports, travel, business, or world events.
Talk about something interesting you love to do. Mention that you're on the volleyball or softball team. Do you play an instrument? Are you artistic? Discuss the amazing trips you've been on or the places you would love to see. Talk about what you do for a living, but avoid making it seem like a job interview. Remember, what we do is not who we are. Sometimes we can get so caught up in our career (I have been guilty of this from time to time) that we forget.

Don't talk about politics, family, religion, the fact that you can barely make your car payment, pop Prozac like it's candy, or that you can't wait to get married. Also, perhaps avoid mentioning you want to have four children or the opposite, and how you can't believe people are still getting married today.
It's about getting to know one another, and determining by the end of the date if this is someone you would like to go out with again.

Your intuition is a helpful guide to depend on. It will lead the way, but the fact of the matter is, you need to trust it. Have you ever had a gut feeling that something didn't feel right about someone? It doesn't need to be a potential love interest. It could even be an acquaintance or stranger who makes you feel uncomfortable. You may not even realize why you feel this way, but the feeling is there. People often go against that little voice inside their head. The few times I've gone against my own intuition and went on a second date anyway, it never worked out. I learned to trust it, because amazingly enough, it usually steers me in the right direction.

So, who pays on a first date?
A simple question with a simple answer: the person who did the asking pays. Generally, it would be the man. If a woman feels bad because she knows she makes a lot more money than her gentleman friend and she wants to contribute, that's fine, but not necessary. I know guys who have been offended when the woman asked to pay the tab on the first date. I know others who would jump for joy if a woman paid. One of my friends let women pay for

first dates if they offered, when he was single. Still, the man usually picks up the bill on the first date and perhaps the first few, if not more. I haven't been asked to split the bill on a date, and only heard of a few women who have encountered this scenario. One of them said the guy actually took out a calculator! For the most part, I feel most men honor this tradition. Men, if you ask a woman on a date, please be a gentleman and take care of the tab. It's a common rule, so please don't act like you forgot it exists. If you cannot afford to date, find someone who isn't wrapped up in dining out and prefers walking, going to the park, picnics, and other low cost options. Your date doesn't need to feel like they should make it through many tests in a certain time frame before they're privileged enough to go to a restaurant that doesn't have golden arches and a playground. On the other hand, don't overextend yourself. Show her the best night possible, but don't date above your means to impress her. As for the ladies, don't order the most expensive item on the menu because you want to eat only the best that "fine" dining has to offer at someone else's expense. Also (this is the latest doozy I've heard), don't ask if you can order another meal to take home to your child! The bottom line is, whoever picks up the bill is doing so as a courtesy, so show you sincerely appreciate it with a simple "thank you" and a smile. Let them know you are genuinely grateful for their hospitality.

Where is a good spot to go on a first date?

Somewhere you can talk and get to know one another is a must. It shouldn't be a place where you need to scream at the top of your lungs to communicate. A movie is not suggested for the opposite reason. There are a variety of ideas for some fun first dates, such as meeting for a drink, a coffee at Starbucks, and having lunch or dinner.

My suggestion is if you don't know each other too well, go for drinks. You'll have a few hours to learn what they're all about. If you like what you see, then you can move on to date #2. If you want it to be short and sweet because you're unsure about him or her, schedule the date right after you get out of work and before you've had time to go home, change, and relax. That's just enough to figure out if this is someone you would like to spend more time with. If you have known the person for a while, dinner is appropriate.

The volunteers had a lot to say about where they would want to go on a first date.

Nearly everyone said they preferred going for a drink, a cup of coffee, or dinner with drinks. Other ideas were: the zoo, mini golf, a comedy club, a long drive, concert, the beach, lunch, dancing, out for ice cream, a motorcycle ride, and a sporting event.

Quite a few said they liked a dinner and a movie. A long walk was another popular response.

A comical answer I read was from a man named Jim (82) who responded, "To a nice place unless she wants to go to a dump."

Do you expect some sort of fireworks on a first date?

Only a small percentage (23 people out of 109, or 21%) feel they do. The greater majority just said, "Go with the flow."

> ### *When asked if they think they expect some fireworks on the first date, male volunteers said:*
>
> "For a girl who may fit my skewed vision of 'girlfriend material,' I expect a solid connection, with enough similar interests that we can come back to for future dates."
>
> "When I'm very attracted to a girl, yes, I think so."

> Sharon (42) made a good point.
> "No, I don't expect fireworks, because people are nervous on first dates and at times can't be completely themselves."

> **Other female volunteers stated:**
>
> "Most likely! I have always been very particular when it comes to dating someone and I expect a great deal of chemistry, or I'm not going to waste my time or theirs."
>
> "Eh, not really. It is only the first date. I usually go in thinking the worst will happen. I hate confrontation and I fear meeting shmucks and weirdoes. I just think sometimes 'fireworks' are overrated. Maybe one day I'll be lucky and experience that great feeling with someone right off the bat, but until then, there will be no real expectations."

A study on dating by Mary Claire Serewicz from the University of Denver and Paul Mongeau of Arizona State University stated first dates are designed to produce several relationship outcomes (such as sexual partner, friendship, short-term relationship, or life partner). The three greatest common goals people have on first dates are: to reduce uncertainty, achieve relational escalation, and to have fun. They found that some signs of a successful first date are: similarities between the two individuals, a goodnight kiss at the end of the date, and holding hands.

In a study done by Alice Eagly and Wendy Wood, both professors of Psychology at Northeastern University, they propose the idea that both men and women are looking for certain attractiveness that fits their taste and style. "The value of attractiveness" stems from its perceived association with the ability to provide sexual pleasure. They stated men seek sexiness and characteristics such as domestic skills, but women place less importance on sexiness and more importance on how courteous the man is (opens the door for her, compliments her, and acts generally considerate). They are also more likely to express companionship, friendship, and romantic relationship goals.

I agree with both studies, but was a bit surprised that men are still placing a strong emphasis on domestic skills. I have dated some great cooks who keep immaculate homes. It's still true. The way to a man's heart is through his stomach.

In 2011, William Cupach, a professor at Illinois State University, and Brian Spitzberg, a professor at San Diego State University, identified that people operate from master narratives, where stories represent our expectations of how things should work, based on common fairytales about the perfect dates others experience. They went on to say people tend to create realities and cultural norms from what the typical first date should be like, and daters need to be cautious of what they say on the first date. Try not to embarrass yourself by telling a story to increase attraction, since it may backfire on you.

You can't go back and erase the damage if you do something bizarre! Don't let your fist date be a "dating disaster!"

Here are some funny "disaster" stories:

> A guy went on a date with a girl he met on the internet. Her profile was well written, she had great pictures and a nice figure. When she arrived for the date, she was pregnant! When questioned on why she didn't tell him about this major change in her life, she gave him a rude look and stated, "Don't you want to be a father?"

> My friend went on a date with a gastroenterologist who she had been talking with for a while. He asked her if she wanted to know why he chose to practice that specific type of medicine, because he gets that question all the time. She said, "Okay, why?" He told her how fascinated he always was with (to put it to you politely) waste products! He continued to go on and on about it. My friend's face told it all. After a short while he stated, "Um, this is not going too well, is it?"

> I once went on a first date that went very well. We had great conversation that flowed effortlessly, had a lot in common, and enjoyed good food and wine. One of my mottos in life is "no drama," which I shared with my date that evening and he seemed thrilled to hear that. At the end of this date I was thinking, "I

would definitely like to see this man again." Fast forward two days later when I received a call from his ex-girlfriend, informing me that she had his phone because he got arrested, and just wanted to let me know. She wasn't trying to "cock-block" him (a term I'd never heard a woman use before), and stated that it is ironic that he had started dating again because they didn't break up too long ago. (He told me he'd broke up with her six months ago.) They had been talking again recently, and also, she said he owed her money! Later that evening, he explained he'd been arrested because he missed a court date for a traffic violation. His ex-girlfriend had his phone because she was watching his dog. I let him know his ex had contacted me, and it was obvious they were still in contact.

Any one of those things would be a deal-breaker, but the fact is, I didn't want any of that drama.

My friend went out with a girl who with a high-powered career. She talked about her stressful job for a while and then went on to ask him a lot of questions about his career. (He also had a prominent position and did very well for himself.) She then went on and on about how easy he must have had it (compared to her) because he is a "white male." He disagreed, saying he didn't grow up in a nice part of town, where he was in the minority. His family didn't have any money, they lived in a trailer park, and he had to put himself through school. She acted like she didn't even hear what he said and kept rambling on and on about injustice for women. She then proceeded to talk about how "out of touch and unfair" he was because he expected his employees to work from either 8–5 or 9–6, because she felt he wasn't being flexible enough. At this point he got up and walked out.

Another friend went on a recent date and when she arrived, her date was dressed in jeans, a t-shirt, and ball cap. (They were at a nice restaurant.) He then said he does not get dressed up until about the third one of "these things." They sat at the bar to eat dinner and were having a few drinks, when he took his gum out of his mouth and put it on his napkin, closest to the side my friend was sitting on. The best part is, after he had finished eating, he put it back in his mouth! She made it through the date without mentioning it. I give her a lot of credit. I don't think I could have pretended this didn't happen, and would have made some funny remark.

A guy was dating a woman for a while and was starting to like her a lot. He saw that she enjoyed drinking but chalked it up to all the drinking they did socially since they got together. He took the next step to invite her to a family party (with her child). At the party, she drank way too much and embarrassed him. He told her that night that he no longer wanted to see her. A short while later he read that she received a D.U.I. Always watch the signs. If the person you're dating needs to drink an overabundance of alcoholic beverages every time you're together, they're not just being social. They might have an addiction.

And the latest: my friend went out on a date recently and had a fantastic time. While they were talking, both discussed recent dates that didn't go too well. His date said she met a guy online and went for a drink. Things were going pretty well until he asked her if she'd like to go to another bar and wouldn't mind driving. When she questioned where his car was, he said he didn't have one. His mother had dropped him off and he is living with his parents because he just got out of jail! She made an excuse for not wanting to go to the next bar, but did give him a ride home. He insisted she come in to meet his parents and then when she tried to leave quickly, her car wouldn't start. Everyone deserves a fresh start, but if he would have disclosed his big news before they met, it would have been up to her to decide if she wanted to go out, and not have been so shocked to hear it in the moment.

Now that you have heard these dating fiasco stories, prevent your first date from being the conversation of someone else's "disaster" story by following the simple steps we have discussed.

Chapter Review.

Fred was out for a morning jog, when he passed a woman he had seen walking on this same route multiple times before. The next day he saw her again, but this time he waved as he went by. She waved back, so he slowed down and started walking beside her.

He asked for her number and if she wanted to meet him for a beer that evening. Myra eagerly agreed to meet at a local sports bar at seven. She arrived at seven on the dot and Fred strolled in at 7:20, claiming he was stuck in traffic.

Myra started chatting up a storm as he ordered two draft beers. Fred matched Myra by cutting into the conversation and talked even more than she did. He went on and on about his all-star days back in high school and how he was the "talk of the town." Myra boosted his already enlarged ego by telling him how impressed she was and someday would love to see pictures from the games his team won because of their star player. They had another beer and Myra took care of the check. As they walked out together Fred told Myra she was "cool" to hang out with. He gave her a fist bump then slapped her backside and laughed. Myra told Fred how funny he was and that she had fun too. They said goodbye and walked to their cars separately.

Bob called Lanie two days after their brunch date and told her what a wonderful time he had. She agreed and they talked for a while. He wanted to make sure he secured a date for either Friday or Saturday night, and asked if she would like to go to dinner, then ice skating.

> Lanie chose Saturday, laughed and said she was twelve years old when last on skates, but was willing to try if Bob promised not to laugh.
>
> He assured her he wouldn't let her fall and admitted he hadn't been on skates in ten years himself, but felt it would be something different they could do together. On Saturday, they arrived at the restaurant at 7:30 pm. Bob told Lanie how nice she looked. She thanked him and smiled. They had great conversation and looked into each other's eyes. They really listened to each other and avoided discussing anything that would be considered too serious or negative. They started to get a sense of each other. At the skating rink, Lanie approached the ice with apprehension, but was ready for a challenge. Bob was a bit unsteady on his feet too and grabbed Lanie's hand as they started skating. They laughed a lot that night and had fun together.
>
> The next day, Bob called and invited her to a comedy show on Wednesday night. They laughed so hard, that at one point Lanie had tears in her eyes. At the end of the night, when walking to her car, he said she was a lot of fun and he felt very comfortable with her. Lanie agreed, saying she has enjoyed his company. They kissed good night and said good bye.

Whether you had a good time on your first date or your friends laughed hard at the story you told about your bizarre evening, hopefully you had fun or at least a good laugh, and are ready to try again.

Let's say we assume you had a great first date. All went well and you're looking forward to seeing them again.

Let's continue and see what happens next!

CHAPTER FIVE

Keeping Your Eye on the Prize

You've been out a few times and things are going well. This stage is a lot of fun, but at times it can be a bit awkward until you get to know the new person in your life and start to feel really comfortable in their presence. If this never happens to you, then all the better. There are stages we all go through in relationships. Each step comes with new bouts of enthusiasm and challenges. In this chapter, we will discuss how a precedent is set right from the start — being true to yourself, dating expectations or the lack thereof, and how to know if the person you're dating is really into you.

The beginning is the honeymoon period filled with excitement. You start to imagine what "could be," and the thought of having someone by your side makes you happy. Women tend to daydream in this stage. You must be cautious to not get too carried away, and keep both feet planted firmly on the ground. Try to pace the relationship so it doesn't rapidly get stale, thereby keeping things new and fresh. As you continue to date, you get more comfortable with each other, and learn more about what the person is made of.

As discussed previously, when it comes to dating, I'm still traditional and think the man should pursue the woman, meaning he should ask her out and act like a gentleman. However, I'm not stuck in a time warp. I feel we are all equal, but this is one area where I think romance and creativity should come into play. The man should relish making the woman happy, and the woman should be pleased he made the effort.

Men, every woman loves a man with a plan. Show her you went out of your way to research some great spots where the two of you can go and make the initial dates convenient for her. You should be the one doing the driving, but she can take her own car to meet you if she prefers. Open her car door, hold doors open for her, and pull out her chair at dinner (if there is no maître d' to do so). Gentlemen already know this, but with today's dating standards, many men don't. Also, some women are not showing how much they appreciate it when a man does these things, which may be why some have stopped. A simple thank you can go far.

If a relationship starts off with the woman doing all the work and calling the man all the time, being content with microwave popcorn and a cable movie, and if she giddily answers her phone at three am, runs over to his apartment to play naked Twister, the bar is set low and the mystery is over.

For those women who want to do all of the above, if that's what you want, then wonderful. But don't seem shocked months afterwards, if you find yourself wishing for a romantic surprise on Valentine's Day. All you'll get is your man on the sofa, beer in hand, laughing because, "Oh boy, Vito's restaurant on the corner is mobbed with people waiting for their table to celebrate a stupid holiday Hallmark created!" There'll be no planned date, card, flowers, and you can forget about any other creative romantic gesture. As I have already discussed a few times, people need to have standards and stick to them.

I want to be clear. Women today are strong and assertive, and should let men know they are interested. They can ask them out, call and text. They know what they want and go after it with vigor, which is very empowering. They just don't need to take over the show and do all the work.

There are some great guys who are being taken advantage of, due to their deep level of kindness. They always seem to have a woman they're trying to "save." She always seems to have a lot of problems she needs him to help her with or rescue from, and bad luck seems to follow her like a shadow. Guys, when you meet a woman surrounded by drama, avoid getting sucked into the excitement. If you crave it, hit your local amusement park and take a ride on the "Tower of Terror" or the triple loop roller coaster, instead of experiencing it while dating.

If you feel you're giving too much too soon, like you're always putting forth more effort than your potential partner, or are behaving in a way you usually wouldn't, bells should ring, making you aware this may not be worth the effort. Relationships are all about give and take, meaning it's two people working together, not just one. The tables obviously won't always be evenly balanced, but they shouldn't be way off kilter, either.

Be true to yourself. It's better to be disliked for being who you are than to be loved for who you're not. If someone doesn't like you, don't bend like a pretzel to meet their approval. Remember, not everyone will like us (for various reasons), even if you did nothing wrong. If we expect everyone to like us and conform to their expectations, we wouldn't be true to ourselves, and our self-worth would suffer as a result.

An incredibly important element I must stress is to be honest with those you date. Be honest about yourself and your life, so you do not start what may end up turning into a relationship with a lie. Allow your date the privilege to get to know the real you. Men, if a friend sets you up with his wife's friend, don't feel you have to appear more successful and compete with your friend. Women, don't say you enjoy camping, when your idea of camping is the Holiday Inn instead of the Hilton.

What types of things do you do to impress someone when initially dating? Do men and women's expectations differ?

The majority of women I questioned said they would dress really nice and look their best. With most men and many women, they said they would simply "be myself." Some of the men said that they try to show they have a good sense of humor.

For example, Mario is a gentleman with a definite plan! When dating someone, Mario always makes sure he has a clean car. If it's a dinner date, he picks the restaurant and makes reservations. He asks the restaurant to place a flower on the table! He usually makes reservations at two restaurants just to make sure everything goes smooth with no hiccups. Impressive.

Another common answer from both sexes was to make sure they "listen" to what their date had to say. A few of the women stated they try not to talk too much. Women usually talk so much more than men, and have to be cognizant not to ramble on and on as their date tries to get in a few words.

When people are initially dating, you learn all about likes, dislikes and routines, and then start to evaluate if you "click" or not.

Do you believe in the three-date rule, where after the third date, the couple is expected to have a hot and steamy night of passion?

Well, out of all the people I questioned, only a few people thought so. Nearly all simply wanted to get to know one another and grab some kisses here and there.

When asked what they expect after making it to date number three, the men asked said:

"On the first three dates, I am only trying to get to know the person as well as I can. I want to make sure this is someone I can make a commitment to before anything physical happens.

"Good conversation and signs of interest."

"The awkwardness should be over and we should be getting into more personal matters. Nothing too revealing, but it should be beyond, 'So where are you from?'

"By now, she should have my number programmed in her cell (though not on speed dial, please), and we'll have groped some, if nothing else."

As a rule, people usually want to have strong attraction before having sex. Some of the guys added "progressing intimacy" was important to deciding when to have sex. Respect, no matter the gender, was of utmost importance.

Ann (49) agreed with sex after the third date, stating, "The first three dates should be good conversation and a good time. After three dates, sex needs to happen."

However, most of the women disagreed.

> ***This is what some of the women I questioned had to say about their expectations after making it to date number three:***
>
> "Respect, humor, light conversation, and no baggage."
>
> "As the song goes, getting to know you, getting to know all about you."
>
> "Respect, great manners, and best behavior. Put effort into appearance. The man should treat for the dates if he asks me out. Get to know each other, ask questions—don't just talk about yourself. Don't try to jump my bones or try to sleep with me so soon."

Now, the next time you make it to date #3, there's no pressure. Unless the lights start to dim, the candles are lit, the massage oil comes out and soft music starts playing in the background. If this is the case, it's then up for you to decide which way to go.

Do people want sex? Of course! But remember this line: slow and steady wins the race. Pace yourself. Both men and women enjoy sex. I don't think there is a man out there who'll disagree with me that they want sex, and having it on the first date is more than fine with them. Men have admitted to me they will try to have sex right away. Some will wait for a while, but it's the woman who determines when.

These same men admitted that even though they try to make women believe they can't, they're capable of waiting.

So, you feel like you've met a great catch. You're having a lot of fun together, talking quite regularly, and you even introduced him to your dog.

How do you know when someone is into you?

I personally feel this one is pretty easy. When the person is making an effort, calling, planning weekly dates, if they seem happy in your presence and ask a lot of questions while listening intently, trying to get to know you better, they're into you.

One of the male volunteers, Okon (49) feels, "It's the way the person talks to you, and the things they do for you that really show how much they care."

Lauren (24) feels, "If they touch me frequently, or make a point to be near me" that shows her the attraction is definitely there.

It is important to show you're into the person, but avoid going overboard. Take your time getting to know the other person and enjoy the quality time together. Relish the newness, the excitement as you await their call and your next date. Think about how much fun you'll both have.

Overall, when someone is into you, you know it because they show it by what they say and how they make you feel. However, make sure they back it up with actions, so it's not only talking the talk, but walking the walk.

Chapter Review.

Three months have gone by.

After their initial meeting, Fred called Myra the following week (after finishing happy hour with his friends one evening). They met for a drink, then went back to his place and engaged in the horizontal mambo, which started a pattern between them. As the weeks passed, Fred fit Myra into his busy schedule when he had time after work, the gym, other women, and time with the guys. He knew if he called,

Myra was always more than happy to oblige to whatever request he had. Due to his lack of commitment, Myra wanted him even more.

She was sure she could tame this bad boy; after all, she had heard about a friend of a friend that had a "friends with benefits" arrangement for a couple of years, and one day this woman's "friend" told her how crazy he was for her.

Myra bought new clothes and changed her hairstyle, but when she invited Fred to go out with other "couples," he always seemed to be busy. She texted him multiple times a day and left cute voice mail messages so he would think about her throughout the day. The majority of the time the messages went unanswered, but whenever Fred and Myra did get together for some fun, he always explained why he was so busy. Myra offered to clean Fred's apartment one day since he had been working so much, thinking she would do the poor guy a favor because he couldn't even fit in time to clean.

At two in the morning, they got together after Fred had hit the clubs with the boys all night. After they had been intimate, Myra told Fred she wanted more. It had been three months and she was sick of sharing him with everybody. Fred went into a song and dance about needing time because of being hurt in the past, and didn't know if he was capable of giving more, but said, "You never know." Myra said she felt bad about the painful relationships he had in the past and assured him she would wait.

Bob and Lanie were seeing each other about two times a week for the past few months. Bob planned some amazing dates and Lanie responded in kind by cooking him dinner a few times. The hours fly by when they're together. They have a lot in common. Both enjoy playing golf, and Lanie admits her game improved since Bob's tips to improve her swing. They met each other's friends, and sometimes get together with them on weekends. Bob and Lanie's friends think they're a great match. She told a friend recently Bob makes her extremely happy, because they communicate very well and he understands her. When they had differing opinions, they make sure they respect what the other has to say. The couple has been pacing the relationship and intimacy is progressing naturally, but slowly. They're instead establishing friendship, trust, and deeper feelings to build a foundation for the relationship. When the time was right they enjoyed a night together, which was very memorable. Recently, Bob talked about having Lanie accompany him to see his parents in a few months.

Lanie's face lit up like a kid at Disney World, but after the thrill wore off, she felt a bit anxious about meeting them, because she wanted everything to go well. He could tell she had something on her mind, and she explained her angst about meeting his parents. Bob wrapped his arms around her and reassured her that his parents were going to love her as much as he does. "I do, I love you Lanie," he proclaimed. "I love you, too," she replied, as they embraced one another.

In 2012, the biological anthropologist Helen Fisher released a study that questioned 6,000 men. The study revealed that men fell in love just as often as women, were just as likely to believe marriage is forever, and many men wanted to settle down. Thirty-one percent of men went as far as to say that they would commit to someone they were not in love with, as long as she had all the other attributes they were looking for in a partner.

I feel both sexes desire happiness and companionship above all. Not everybody feels this way, but a great majority of people do. Some will want it at different points in their life, some will have an "ah-ha" moment and know when they are ready, while others were ready for as long as they can remember, always searching for someone with whom they can share the journey we call life.

CHAPTER SIX

Two Halves are Better Than One

You're happy. You feel like a kid experiencing a crush for the first time. Right now, he or she can do no wrong. You feel like you're living in a utopia, a natural high that feels oh-so-good.

Let's look at how our brain reacts to love (lighting up like a Lite-Brite screen) and the stages of commitment. Next, we will be looking at some of the essential components of a relationship such as: personal space, compromise, sex, intimacy, and trust. As we discuss each component we will also take a good look at difficulties that may arise as you maneuver your way through each of these areas.

Our body produces chemicals that make us act giddy or "head over heels," excited at the mere touch of our new love interest. When a person falls in love, the ventral tegmental area in the brain floods the caudate nucleus with dopamine. The caudate then signals for more dopamine; the more dopamine, the higher a person feels. The same system becomes activated when someone takes cocaine. So, it's like you're walking around in a drug-induced love daze. See why this is called the honeymoon period? When you first start dating, everything is new, fresh, and filled with excitement. Although it's different for everyone, it primarily lasts for roughly thirty months. Due to this fact, the longer people wait to get married, the better. That's why I tell people who decide to marry after less than a year together to proceed with caution. In September of 2014 Andrew M. Francis and Hugo M. Mialon, professors from Emory University, surveyed over 3,000 people across the U.S. who were either married or had been at some point in their life. They found that people who married within the first six months of meeting were most likely to divorce, and couples who dated for at least three years before marrying had the highest probability of staying together. The results of this study mirrored the results from a similar study done in 2006. When someone looks at a new love, the neural circuits usually associated with social judgment are suppressed. One may make choices during this time they wouldn't normally make. So, if you feel the desire to run off to Vegas to marry someone you've known for three days or three months for that matter, blame it on your brain, and take a trip with your friends instead!

When you've been dating someone for a while, how do you ensure that you both are on the same page, you both are actually a couple, and don't want to date anyone else?

You know what they say about the word assume: <u>don't</u>, or you'll make an "ass/u/me." This one can be tough. One volunteer, Paul (70) simply stated, "You will know!"

Well, here goes: the most common answer for knowing if you both were on the same page was either: after we have "the talk" (about the current status of the relationship), selected by 44%, closely followed by 39% stating, "When they start to call me their girlfriend/boyfriend." A lot of the men said they were sure when they're having sex regularly. I even got a, "After the first time we have sex." Some of you might read that and think, really? The person who said it was 68, but even today, there are individuals who feel sex, or "making love" is very special, and giving themselves to another means that they are now committed.

Other popular answers were: when they start spending a lot of time with one another, focus exclusively on one another, meet the friends and family—and when at least one day in the weekend is being spent together. Someone even said, "After the third date."

The women were more guarded with their answers because most seem to be taking the man's lead on this one.

Colleen (29) feels that it's when the guy says they are a couple, because she made the mistake of "assuming" and it didn't turn out so well.

Lynn (45) answered, "I thought I used to know the answer, but until a guy says 'we are exclusive,' it doesn't mean a thing."

Women are more apt to jump into relationships, whereas men would rather ease into one. Everyone is different, but most people certainly won't consider they are in an exclusive relationship after only a few dates, and don't assume that after sex you two are an item, either. That's why it's important to take time to know one another before sex, especially if it's someone you're serious about and can envision having a future with. One of my favorite sayings is, "A man for all seasons," which I saw on a billboard in NYC and just had to take a picture. You could say a "woman for all seasons" as well, but the meaning behind the message is to see someone through all "seasons" (or longer) before you decide to commit the rest of your life with them. I hope a lot of you reading this aren't saying to yourself, "Well, too late now. I wish I thought about that when I was falling hard (like a boulder off a cliff for some) after two months of dating Prince Charming or Ms. Philanthropist." This isn't written in stone, since some couples who marry after knowing each other a short while have relationships that work. Overall, however, a greater number of relationships last over the years when they take the time to know one another before getting serious, preferably stretching it for at least two years.

I was married at a young age. My ex-husband pressured me to get married after six months when I suggested we wait at least a year. Not knowing anything about "a man for all seasons" back then, I went along with it because he did his best to sweep me off my feet, and I thought he was my knight in shining armor. Immediately and within the next few years, one serious issue after another presented itself. I began to see through the facade and I tried to make it work, because my vows meant the world to me, and the very thought of divorce devastated me. I was smart enough to know that I needed and deserved a healthy marriage. Had I waited longer before saying "I do," there would have been no way these issues would have been hidden for so long. I probably would have broken up with him before getting married. Do I regret my marriage? I would have to say no, because I live my life without regret. It was my choice at the time and I learned a lot from that relationship. Having not mastered my communication skills at the time (this was also before I became a therapist), I threatened to leave more than once, because I didn't know what else to do. Eventually, I left for a few days, and then came back when enticed with promises of change, but the relationship reached its demise shortly afterward. Toxicity doesn't just magically disappear when it's someone's way of life. Lots of people are not capable of change, even though the thought may cross their mind.

A friend's girlfriend had a strong desire to get married. She dated different guys but never found "the one," and eventually ended up connecting with someone she knew from high school on Facebook. They started a long-distance relationship, and in eight months they were married. Less than two years later, they were divorced. When you have a long-distance relationship, the brief moments spent together are exhilarating. You feed off the excitement of having missed one another and everything is magical. Fast forward to a dose of reality when the honeymoon period ends, which will happen, just like for couples living near one another. When this couple started their relationship, we might as well call it "vacationing with one another." They were stealing bits of time flying to see one another, exploring each other's home base and each other, going out to eat, hanging with friends, etc. When this honeymoon period ends, not only does the couple have to deal with the reality of real life, such as bills, problems, different work schedules, to-do lists and possibly children, but they're also hit with the ins and outs of seeing one another on a regular basis verses bi-weekly, monthly, bi-monthly or whatever amount of time they were used to. It is essential to eventually continue the relationship in the same zip code or at least within driving distance to ensure synchronicity, so you're able to see one another frequently, living your lives and facing problems as they arise. Sometimes it works. The couple is thrilled to finally be together, proving they really are meant to be. In a great majority of cases, such as above, they aren't so lucky, because the relationship didn't have adequate time to gel, slowly progressing through the different stages and experiencing all the ins and outs of real time together from the start.

My friend's sister started off a relationship from afar (two different states). They met online and even had a child together, but sadly, the relationship ended after a few short years. I also know two couples who started out as long-distance relationships and are very happily married today. They made it work because eventually one of them moved and experienced life as a couple regularly.

So, if the two of you have enjoyed all four seasons, have the utmost respect for one another, live within driving distance and enjoy each other's company—you're off to a great start, geographically and emotionally.

It looks like for my volunteers, the main consensus between the sexes is this: they agree that when they don't want to see anyone else, you're actually in a committed relationship.

The Relationship Institute in Michigan came up with stages of a committed relationship, and although some will skip a stage or two, others will experience all the stages. The following list is a guide to common themes experienced when you're engaged in a committed relationship. Although I didn't list the full description of each stage, I focused on the main themes they described:

ONE: Romantic Love

This is the love that Hollywood loves to promote as the only kind of love. Romantic love is wonderful, easy, and effortless. It is very spontaneous and alive. The feelings and perceptions that go through both people are that we are one—we are the same. I can give and receive love with little or no effort required. There is a tremendous emphasis on maximizing similarities and minimizing differences. There is generally a high degree of passion, and feelings and expressions of romance come easily and often. The partners think about each other constantly, make ample eye contact, and are very affectionate when together. Many people experience this as living in a state of near-constant bliss and infatuation. There is a belief that these feelings and experiences will go on forever. However, this stage generally lasts from six months to two years, and is the shortest of any of the stages of long-term committed relationships.

TWO: Adjusting To Reality

Ah, reality. Inevitably, predictably and eventually, reality rears its ugly head, and the bubble bursts on the romantic stage. Sometimes it's a slow leak, other times it's a sudden and complete blowout. But either way, something happens which causes a minor or major conflict in the new relationship. Sometimes the trigger is living together, having to share household chores, and experiencing personal habits up close. Sometimes it is an act of deception which is discovered, or it's planning a wedding, buying a house or sharing finances. Whatever the cause, after the conflict occurs, it becomes impossible to continue the fantasy that this person and this relationship are immune from struggle, effort, and reality. Differences which were previously obscured suddenly become visible. Conflicts, anxieties, disappointment and hurt replace the effortless flow of the Romantic stage. There is a sense this person is not living up to your hopes and dreams, and an accompanying loss of closeness.

There is a desire to be close again, but there's confusion as how to create that closeness. It is the first time that fears of intimacy begin to arise. Suddenly, the couple must learn how to deal with very real differences, with conflict, and how to integrate being an independent person, as well as someone in an intimate relationship.

In short, Adjusting to Reality is the stage where the real relationship begins.

THREE: The Power Struggle

As the disillusionment of the Adjusting to Reality stage deepens, the couple tends to have more disagreements. Minor issues blow up into larger arguments. Yelling appears for the first time, if it ever will. Both partners dig in their heels and fiercely defend their positions on issues. This once tender, effortless, loving relationship has become a battleground that evolved into a daily Power Struggle. It's typical in the development of a long-term committed relationship.

For the first time in the relationship, there are occasional, or for some—frequent thoughts of leaving the relationship. This person who recently appeared to be the embodiment of pure love and joy in your eyes suddenly seems self-centered and untrustworthy. Doubts arise as to whether the other person really loves you. There are consistent feelings of ambivalence and anger. Each partner is afraid of giving in, and wants the other to change. This is where deep resentments begin to form, which if left unchecked, becomes a cancer that eventually eats away at all the love and tenderness.

This doesn't have to be the end of the relationship. The tasks for the couple here are to develop problem-solving, conflict resolution and negotiating skills. They must learn to support their partner's own growth, even if they feel it compromises their own. They may even see the origins of the patterns of their conflicts, and their dysfunctional ways of resolving them in their family of origin.

FOUR: Re-Evaluation

The Power Struggle is physically and emotionally draining, and if the couple can survive, they move into the next stage, the conscious re-evaluation of their relationship. Whereas the original commitment is typically based on projections of fantasy, this re-evaluation considers the reality, fears and defenses of each person. You know more about who this person is now, their limitations, and if they are capable of improving or getting better. Knowing all that, do you still want to stay? That is the question that gets answered during this stage. As a result, strong fears of abandonment come up. Can I make it by myself? Am I really okay the way I am? Will anyone else find me attractive or appealing?

Both people emotionally (and sometimes physically) disengage and withdraw during this stage. It's when separation, divorce and/or an affair are most likely to occur. Feelings of resentment are less intense in this stage, and are replaced by a numb feeling of being very flat and empty.

Sometimes, an affair begins at this stage, and then it can be almost impossible for the relationship to recover. The primary relationship has too little going for it in the way of gratification on either side, so the affair will seem shiny, new and exciting, compared to the old relationship. Each person must stay present and honor their commitment, develop individually, and be able to see their partner as a separate person. This is essential for the relationship to survive and move into the next stage.

FIVE: Reconciliation

In this stage, after the distance caused by the re-evaluation and if the relationship has endured to this point, there is a re-awakening of interest in getting closer and re-connecting. Knowing what they know is coming from reality and not fantasy, each partner now possesses a willingness to try once again.

Both accept the conflicts and differences, but approach them with a different attitude, using them as opportunities for learning about oneself and the other, and act as catalysts for growth and change. They recognize the differences are real and won't go away, and neither person can change the other. Thus, begins a process of struggling to create an honest, genuine intimate relationship. This relationship then begins to produce satisfaction for both.

There is a deeper level of acceptance in this stage because you worked at your relationship. The war is over and now your life can be nurtured in a loving, accepting relationship. There was a sincere desire to learn, and you did, because you worked through the issues to a satisfying resolution.

SIX: Acceptance

The final stage in a committed relationship, which researchers estimate less than 5% of couples ever reach, is one of complete Acceptance. There is an integration of the need of the self and the needs of the relationship. Each person takes responsibility for their own individual lives, and providing support for their partner. A high level of warmth is present. The couple maintains a balance between autonomy and union. Conflicts still arise on occasion, but as a result of former struggles, the couple has figured out how to resolve most conflicts relatively quickly. Resentments are few. They work together as a team to stay connected, while maintaining their own identities.

Making it to the Acceptance stage is a lot of work. Communication, conflict resolution, compromise, and love are all embroiled in your strong union at this point, making you cherish what you have built together even more, so the love can continue to grow every day.

It's disheartening that only less than 5% of couples make it to the Acceptance stage. So, what does that say about the majority of couples? People are letting their "egos" get in the way. They're so busy thinking about what they should be doing, what others think, expect and do, and what they're missing out on, that they don't work on growing in mind, body, and spirit with the one person who is supposed to matter most. I feel strongly that if questioned, a great majority of people would say they would like to be in a happy, healthy, relationship, but sadly, most don't know what this looks like.

Now that we have thoroughly explored commitment, let's look at events in the typical dating relationship that will occur at different points over time.

Meeting those most dear to you.

After you have been a couple for quite some time, it is inevitable that friends and family will start to ask when they're going to get to meet this great person you've been talking about and spending so much time with. Most people place a high level of importance on these meetings because they want everyone to have respect and admiration for their new mate.

I usually see someone exclusively for quite some time before I chose to introduce them to friends and especially to family, because this ups the ante on the serious scale. Christi (50) stated it would take more than a year for her to introduce a guy she is seriously dating to her family. Lauren feels it's only appropriate to introduce them if you are considering marriage. Dave (33) feels okay after the first month or two. Mario has a little girl so he wants to wait five or six months, since she will be the girl he wants to stay with for the next forty years.

Meeting the family was pretty serious business for most people.

Those who felt they needed family and friends approval of their partner were only a slightly higher group than those who rely on their own internal voice to make their decision. This became roughly a 60/40 split. Some agreed that it would be great if their family and friends approved of their choice but it was not a deal breaker. If they don't care for the person you are seeing, however, problems can arise. Many parents are very skeptical when it comes to anyone initially dating their son or daughter. For some, no one is good enough in their eyes. Also, watch out for friends of the opposite sex who may secretly wish they were in the other guy or girl's shoes. As jealousy takes over, they may not approve of anyone you date. When you're the one being introduced to your partner's friends and family, it's important for you to try your hardest (even when you need to work extra hard to accommodate their idiosyncrasies) to get along with them. I'm not saying to pretend you're someone else, but consider treating the situation with kid gloves and try to embrace these individuals. Your relationship will be smoother if everyone gets along (and you'll get extra points from your sweetheart and perhaps more "loving").

This is my space and that is yours.

Do you want to run away when someone comes on too strong?

The results to this question were very close. Fifty seven percent of my respondents felt the urge to run when the person they're dating starts coming on strong, but the other 43% welcomed the attention. Men especially, said they would be flattered. Paul feels it's exciting when a woman comes on strong. Michael (45) from Florida said he would end up running if he wasn't into her, and that was the general consensus among the men. However, if they liked her, "bring it on." The men who said they would be more likely to run wanted things to happen over time, and didn't want anyone that appeared needy or desperate. The greater majority of ladies said they would run for cover if a man came on too strong.

Donna (42) said, "I don't like it when guys are too forward. Makes me think they are such a perv!"

"I had a boyfriend when I was nineteen who was constantly talking about getting married," Rachel said. "Within two months I broke up with him."

Even if you're lonely, don't know anybody in town, and find yourself talking to your cat on Saturday night, you should still "appear" to have a life. Do you know why parents wait in line in the middle of the night to get one of the hottest toys of the holiday season? Because everyone wants it, that's why! So, act as if anyone would be lucky to have you as a partner, and strut your stuff!

Personal space for Americans is usually an arm's length away, come any closer and people feel uncomfortable. In many other countries when regarding their culture, it deviates considerably from much closer to farther away when conversing with someone.

What about space in a relationship? How much personal time and space does one need?

I think it's different for every couple. One thing to consider: it's healthy to have personal time to yourself and to do what's important to you, whether it is reading a book, working out, riding your bike, relaxing and so on. Don't let anyone ever make you feel guilty for having "alone" time. When someone badgers you for wanting that time because they can't bear to spend five minutes by themselves, then it's, "HOUSTON, WE HAVE A PROBLEM."

Togetherness is great and two can be better than one, but you also need to be two separate, healthy halves that come together as one whole. I had clients tell me they can't go to the bathroom without their child pounding on the door, wanting to come in, or clients who don't have any friends because their partner will not "allow" them to go out without them. Boundaries need to be established from the start. I believe in any relationship, precedent is established early. From the start, it should be apparent that you have a full life made up of different needs.

Everyone I queried felt personal space was a very significant part of a relationship. Women vouched for more personal time than men. Donna felt that without personal space, the relationship is "Down the tube!"

Todd (37) said, "I feel each person needs to have space fairly often so they don't feel they are 'trapped' in the relationship."

It's an unhealthy sign of insecurity if your partner resists you having any time away. It shouldn't be seen as flattering. Your life should consist of many different pieces, with no one piece or person taking up all your energy.

Let's make a deal.

Compromise is an essential component in a successful relationship. How far are you willing to bend? Are you willing to bend like a rubber band, or is it your way or the highway?

I will never forget one of my favorite lines from the movie, *When Sally Met Harry*. They interviewed a handful of real couples who had been together for many years and one elderly woman said it best; "I gave a little. He gave a little. We got along." Making one another happy by doing what the person liked to do, even if it isn't something you ever thought you would do, is compromise at its best. The longer people are on their own, the more they get set in their ways, and the more they must learn to adjust to be in a relationship.

Volunteers said they are willing to compromise, as long as it doesn't go against their strong beliefs or morals. A few feel like they compromised too much and have been taken advantage of, while others admitted to compromising more at the beginning of a relationship. There naturally are things both you and your partner like to do, and others you have no interest in, but at times, you need to partake in activities that aren't your first choice, to show your love. You never know when you might enjoy doing something new, after all. You're not going to agree on everything, of course, but appreciating the other person's viewpoint demonstrates that you value their opinion.

In 2011, Mark White, chair of the Department of Philosophy at the College of Staten Island, stated that compromise is great in small doses and often necessary to smooth over a few rough edges of an otherwise well-functioning relationship. He said it is when we start compromising essential elements like needs, wants, and our deepest desires, that cracks show up in the foundation of that relationship. When partners can't find a way to satisfy both needs at the same time, they often start to resent having to satisfy the need of the other person, as their needs go unfulfilled, and that causes slow-burning anger and pain.

I completely agree. If you feel you're going against who you are or what you're opposed to so that your partner can be happy, eventually you will resent them and continue to have an unsettling feeling. Hopefully, this will spark you to redress the situation and work it out. You want a partner who respects your point of view, even if they're not in total agreement with what you think or how you feel. They might be willing to agree to disagree, so both parties are able to do what they want, within limits.

Research by social psychologists from Berkeley revealed that sacrificing for someone you love will show you care, and make you feel good about yourself. The studies showed that if you find you're the one who is constantly sacrificing or forced to sacrifice, be cautious. Sacrifice is a hallmark of an intimate relationship, but shouldn't lead to neglecting your needs. The right kind of sacrifice can unite people and strengthen the relationship, but if you continuously suppress your true wants, eventually, thoughts of separating are inevitable.

Good communication early on sets patterns for the future. Imagine both of you on the same team versus different teams. It's not a competition. I have seen people who want things to go their way so badly, they end up jeopardizing their relationship.

In marriage or in a serious relationship, couples simply must learn to work as a team, especially when children come along. In July 2013, a study by Baylor University found apologizing wasn't the key to a successful relationship, but relinquishing some of the power to the other person was. Earlier studies said there are two basic types of underlying concerns couples experience during conflicts: "perceived threats," where the person thinks his or her status is threatened by a "critical" or "demanding" partner, and "perceived neglect," where an individual sees a partner as being disloyal, inattentive, or not giving enough time into the relationship. I love Dr. Gary Chapman's book *The Five Love Languages*, and have recommended it to couples I have worked with. It focuses on figuring out your partner's "love language" so you can meet them where they are. If both partners figure out what is most important to their partner, there will be smoother sailing ahead.

Let's talk about sex.

Some of you may be thinking, this is getting good! Sorry to disappoint, we're not going to get into various positions or new things you can do to spice up your sex life, although that would be interesting. Let's talk about how long to wait before having sex (versus a one-night stand).

Is it possible to have sex too soon?

There were a wide range of answers as to how long people wait. Anywhere from the third or fourth date (a popular answer, especially among men), to more than six months. Twenty-nine percent felt sometime in the first month seems right, and close behind, 25% felt two to three months was more likely. Then, a tie at 13% said four to six months, and 13% felt six to twelve months was the magic time frame. The remaining 20% said that it was best for when the couple is ready, trust has been formed, and no one feels pressured. A few people felt a couple should wait until they are married. Bruno (28) said he leaves it to the girl to decide and when she holds out, it really impresses him, since it shows she respects herself, and sees him to be a long-term deal.

Everyone agreed that sex is an integral part of a relationship and the greater majority think you can have sex too soon. More women felt this way than men. A small percentage of men felt you couldn't have it too soon and there was only one who was still on the fence. It's like climbing a ladder. Unless you just need a stepladder to grab something quick, you have to climb many steps before you get to the top. Brandon (35) said, "Sometimes it may be too soon if you didn't get to know them well enough. Sex sometimes makes things serious fast."

Sonia (25) said, "Yes, I think you can have sex too fast and it has happened to me. Sex can change a relationship. It's important to be on the same page as the person you are dating before you have sex."

Other comments included: "Sex can affect a relationship negatively if you are not ready for it" and "If you are not a good match, it can quickly end things if you don't have the time and emotion to back it up and work through it."

Here is also what Rachel, a twenty-one-year old from Charleston, had to say; "I believe you can have sex too soon, mostly because of the double standard that is set up for women to fail. Have sex too soon and you're a whore, but if you wait until you're comfortable, you're a prude, and if you pressure someone into having sex, they're eventually going to resent it, which will eventually cause a rift in the relationship."

A friend who knew I was writing this book told me he agrees that women should wait as long as they can before they have sex. He went on to say, "If a woman jumps in bed with a guy after their first date and then tells him, 'You are so special, I've never done this before,' it may very well be true, but she is almost better off saying nothing. He won't believe it anyway." He told me the guy will go for it, but nine out of ten times she won't be the girl he eventually brings home to meet his parents. Maybe you think it sounds unfair or so 1950s, but it's true. A double standard does still exist when it comes to sex, whether we admit it or not. There are definitely couples who had sex on the first date and the relationship continued on from there, but statistics prove they have less of a probability of making it to their golden wedding anniversary. I'm also not saying women don't want sex. Of course they do. If you want to go out one night, get your groove on and have a one-night stand, be safe, and it's your choice! Just keep in mind he may not end up being "the one."

Sex brings the relationship to a different level (especially for women), and if you hardly know the person you are sleeping with, it can bring the relationship to a place that one or both people may not be ready to go. Try to wait until you both have agreed to be in a monogamous relationship before you start sleeping together. Try to pace the relationship. Good things really do come to those who wait.

Getting to know someone inside and out on many different levels before becoming physical will deepen your relationship, and if you realize you're not compatible, there's nothing lost, and you've gained knowledge and perhaps a friend.

Prior to the 1960s, couples had pre-marital sex, but not like they do today. Before birth control and the sexual revolution, the thought of having sex with someone may have been enticing, but a lot more was at stake. Men took their time and courted the woman they were interested in, and women relished in being sought after and treated like ladies. Only after dating for a considerable amount of time in a serious relationship or post marriage, would sex enter the picture. Why? Without the luxury of birth control putting their minds at ease, an enjoyable night of passion could lead to pregnancy, which was also not taken lightly. If a young, unmarried, woman ended up pregnant, she would not be celebrated, and likely ostracized.

Research has found that holding off on sex for a while makes for a more satisfying and stable relationship in the future. Dean Busby of Brigham Young University's School of Family Life and his colleagues recruited 2,035 heterosexual adults, whose average age was thirty-six, and were in their first marriages. Participants reported when they and their spouse initially had sex, and answered questions about communication, relationship satisfaction and stability. They were grouped as either having early sex (before dating, or less than one month after they started dating), late sex (between one month and two years of dating), and there was a group who waited until marriage to have sex. The relationships in which people wait the longest to have sex fared the best. Those who had sex before the one-month mark had the worst results. Couples who waited to become sexual had time to figure out how trustworthy their partner was, how well they communicate, and whether they share the same values or not.

In an article by Brett and Kate McKay, the couple explained how delayed intimacy can benefit your relationship. During sex, oxytocin largely increases and peaks during climax. After climax, however, the levels dramatically drop off. To better break things down, dopamine is what drives you to want to have sex and oxytocin draws you to an individual. After climax, your desire for the person dissipates. Thus, instead of making lovers feel closer, sex can actually make partners feel further apart, and even discouraged and restless. They conclude that frequent, comforting feelings strengthen our bonds to one another and make us feel safe. Bonding behaviors and attachment, or "us time," like a soothing touch, comforting one another, eye gazing, and so on, practiced daily, creates a flow of oxytocin which makes it easier to sustain a long-term relationship. When you engage in a sexual relationship early on, you will not have a strong non-sexual stream of oxytocin flowing to compensate for the hormone drop-off post-climax, which may make your relationship feel bumpier, tense, and volatile. If you wait (and don't quickly jump into bed together) until your non-sexual oxytocin steam is running full blast, this flow will smooth over the neurochemical ups and downs that accompany sex so that intimacy enriches your relationship, drawing you closer instead of apart.

As humans, we try everything from a one-night stand or waiting until after a few dates, to a few months or more to have sex. Even though research shows couples who wait the longest usually last the longest, I can't say your relationship will be guaranteed to last if you wait. It will just be given a better chance. Consider how liberating it would be to date someone for a few months without having sex. You will start to build a foundation, then finally unite for that special night of passion. Hopefully, it will feel more special to both.

In a recent article in the Archives of Sexual Behavior, the sexual regrets of both women and men, compiled by researchers over three different studies, were discussed. They queried college students in one study, men and women of different ages in the next, and included a much larger sample in the third which included gays and bisexuals, which was similar to the second study. Fifty-five percent of men regretted not showing someone how sexually attracted they were to them, and 48% regretted not being more sexually adventurous when they were younger. On the other hand, 43% of women regretted how many sexual encounters they had and how everything "moved too fast," with 41% feeling bad about losing their virginity to the wrong person.

Most people explore their sexuality, enjoy sexual encounters and experimenting, and have an appetite for sex. Enjoy your sex life and when you're ready for a deep passionate relationship with someone you truly care about, maybe give abstinence a try for a bit longer than usual, so you hold out for something worth waiting for.

Years ago, I polled some of my male family members and friends about this topic and some other issues, such as, if a man had the opportunity to have a one- night stand with someone they were attracted to, it was guaranteed he wouldn't get caught, how many men would cheat? The answer: <u>more than 90%.</u> I blame it on man's innate need to spread his seed (sorry, guys!), and the fact that many men have a hard time thinking about being with one woman for the rest of their lives. Many do decide to marry and women love them for it. As a bonus: it has been proven people who are married live longer, which is quite interesting.

What about INTIMACY?

I describe intimacy as letting someone into your private world, that space you hold sacred, where they know the deepest parts of you. It's being at ease, experiencing comfort, and a feeling of "being at home" with someone. A loving and intimate relationship is solidified by actions, not only mere words. A soft touch, that glance into your lover's eyes that says so much more than words ever could, accompanied by passionate love making on a lazy morning. Intimacy is based on a certain level of trust; believing that the other person will be there for you, no questions asked.

Some crave it; some can only take so much of it. There are those who have deep rooted issues surrounding intimacy, and those who show us the best examples of what intimacy is all about.

Do a great number of people have a problem with intimacy?
What's your guess?

Apparently, people do: seventy-six people answered yes, versus thirty-three people who feel intimacy is not a common problem.

Elizabeth (19) said she believes they do, but the vast majority of people are too ashamed and embarrassed to admit it, for fear that their significant other will see them as having something wrong with them.

Rachel feels that problems with intimacy stem from issues with insecurity, and I agree. You must be truly secure and have the ability to trust in any relationship, to be completely open and intimate with one another.

Dave feels, "People have been hurt in the past and build up walls. Most people are afraid to let their walls down and be vulnerable. However, without being vulnerable, one will never know love. I guess dating is a slow destruction of the walls to get to know the inner person." Beautifully said.

Most of us learn about intimate relationships from our parents. Our ability to form healthy attachments started with them. If you did not bond to a parent or caregiver in the first three years of your life, with the first year being the most crucial, you will most likely have, or have had problems with loving relationships. A secure attachment to a parent, predominantly the mother, paves the way for healthy, trusting, relationships. This relationship starts even before we are welcomed into the world and let out our very first cry. It's constructing a solid base, like the foundation when building a house. We learn to communicate in a loving or unloving manner, by watching our parents or their significant other interact with one another in a loving or dysfunctional manner, and accept it as normal. Like someone who grew up watching their father abuse their mother and swore they would never enter a relationship like their parents, only to fall in love with an abuser, or becoming the abuser unconsciously. If you pay attention to family patterns you will learn a lot. I work with families where dysfunctional patterns repeat themselves from one generation to the next until someone makes a conscious effort to change and thereby stop the dysfunction. If you want to learn a great deal about someone you're interested in becoming more serious with, pay particular attention to the relationship they have with their parent of the opposite sex. The relationship a man has with his mother or a woman has with their father becomes an example for future relationships. These early relationships become a blueprint when choosing future partners. Even if on a conscious level you realize the example they showed wasn't healthy, your mind can Jedi-mind-trick you with the familiar, and you find yourself questioning, "How did that happen?" We are automatically and unconsciously drawn to what is familiar. No doubt you have heard the term "Daddy's girl" or "Mamma's boy." Or, "If you want to know how a guy is going to treat you, pay attention to how he treats his mother." Then there's, "I don't think there is a woman on earth that could measure up to his mother." We seek out what is comfortable and what we know. Through our adult relationships, we also may attempt to recreate what we desperately wanted to happen in the past, but it never did, without even realizing it. It can be a case of trying to "right the wrong" over and over again, hoping to change a negative pattern that was started at home in childhood with one or both of our parents/caregivers.

A theory that lives on.

Erik Erikson, a German psychoanalyst, came up with the psychosocial theory of development, which considers the impact of external factors, parents, and society on personality development from childhood to adulthood. According to Erikson's theory, every person must pass through a series of eight interrelated stages over their entire life cycle. Intimacy Versus Isolation is the sixth stage of his theory of psychosocial development. This stage takes place during young adulthood between the ages of approximately nineteen and forty, where the major conflict centers on forming intimate and loving relationships with other people. If successful, it leads to strong relationships, and failure usually results in loneliness and isolation.

Just because someone had many negative experiences with love, a traumatic childhood or feels all alone in the world, and like no one seems to "get them," they're not doomed to be alone forever. Some people think love should be a challenge. It needs to be hard and if it isn't, it's too good to be true. If things are flowing naturally and easily, they feel uneasy. I recently read a quote; "Fall in love with someone that doesn't make you think love is hard." Love doesn't need to be difficult. Falling in love should be amazing! We all have the capability to grow personally and/or spiritually, to strive to become a better person as we evolve through our life. Every one of us has been hurt at some point and if it hasn't happened to you yet, you're fortunate, but as with life, it's just a matter of time before you feel disappointment from someone you love. We are human and far from perfect. Everyone's experience is different. We learn many of life's lessons through pain, which often pushes us in a direction that we need to take, like a road map leading the way to where you're ultimately supposed to end up. The deepest souls live many lifetimes in just a single life and have indeed learned immense lessons in the process. To be free of pain that may be haunting you, to heal the broken bond you had/have with a parent, or from failed relationships that created your negative viewpoint toward love, you can choose to work your way through the weeds by reflecting on those experiences. Eventually, it can lead to walking together with someone through a glorious garden.

The one common factor to every failed relationship you ever had is you. I'm not saying you are to blame, but this is where you need to start. Look at every serious relationship you've ever had and try to pick out patterns. Notice the negative aspects of those relationships and see if you can pick out common themes, evident in the way you communicated in each one. Also, pay attention to if you're picking partners with the same communication styles. If it seems like you keep dating the same type and it always ends the same way, you probably are to blame. Don't waste another ten years doing the same thing. They might have a different zip code, look, smell, and voice, but they're often the same type inside. We often pick partners with a communication style similar to one of our parents, because they taught us how to communicate. We walk around with the voice of our mothers and fathers echoing in our heads — sometimes unconsciously, and those ideas, learned responses and patterns affect our loving relationships, parenting styles, and so on.

As so many of you already know, our parent's way was not necessarily the right way, and the negative patterns numerous people have learned when communicating have to be tweaked, pruned, and sometimes even re-learned so you can have healthier relationships and greater overall life satisfaction.

If you get irritated very easily and fly off the handle, yelling at everyone you date after you feel comfortable with them, then walk around saying, "I got that from my mother. She always screamed at my father, my brothers and me, every day when I was growing up." That doesn't cut it. You're using a negative learned behavior as an excuse to continue the destructive pattern. You need to take it a step further and learn ways to relax to start communicating more effectively. You can't continue to blame your parents, who in most cases did the best they could with what they had to work with, or blame anyone else you can think of.

On the flip side, there are parents who displayed a lot of love and warmth, and are great communicators. These parents deserve praise because ultimately, their children benefit. Parenting is the hardest job one will ever have. If your parents have been happily together for many years, you may want to look at what they've been doing to remain in marital harmony, year after year. The bliss isn't in the wedding, it's in the ability to keep love alive.

Everyone has preconceived notions about love. If your role models were substandard, then you may have learned at a very young age that love brings pain. You would be surprised how many memories have been tucked away deep inside, that we carry with us; they contain lost messages about love which you can recover. Here are some examples: "I'm not worthy of love," "People in relationships always lie," and other similar sayings. Write down messages you uncover from childhood and revisit them. Do you believe them to be true? Challenge your thoughts.

Just trust me.

Trust is learned from experiences. So, when someone says, "You can trust me," remember that it needs to be earned. The foundation of any core relationship is built on trust. If you have had one negative experience in your life after another, it is safe to say that it will take you longer to trust than someone who has only had positive experiences. People enter relationships with preconceived notions about love, but some people scrutinize what their partner is doing or how their partner is acting, fearing the worst intentions. If you are always waiting for the ball to drop, thinking they may cheat on you when they're not by your side, it's a recipe for failure. It's important to try to remember that both men and women truly want to make their partners happy, and most don't have interior motives for doing so. Try to change your thoughts about love and replace them with new, positive thoughts if you want to be happy. You need to come to a place of true resolve and I assure you, once you do, it will feel like a weight has been lifted. Not everyone is going to try to break your heart, and once you work through your old baggage and show up with your brand-new suitcase, the sky's the limit!

People want the one they love to feel like they can't live without them. To be the best possible partner in any relationship, you first need to be your "best self," and whole-heartedly love all aspects of yourself! How can you expect someone to love you completely, when you don't love yourself completely? Think about it. We are our own worst enemies. There will be days when you or your partner may not feel 100% self-assured, and perhaps about the relationship as well, but just continue to aim high.

Men tend to equate intimacy with sex, whereas women associate it with love. I feel for men, because ever since they're old enough to dress themselves, they're taught to "be strong," "don't cry," and the old, "while I'm away, you're the man of the house," all while this three-foot-tall "man" is still asking his mom to take the cut the crust off his peanut butter sandwich. Real men do cry and maybe if more did, less would be dying from heart attacks at a young age from the act of suppressing their emotions. Men, if you allow yourself to be more in tune with your feelings and be not afraid to show your softer side, it will open new levels in your relationship. Some men are very emotional, sensitive and in tune with their feelings, but society pressures them to mask those feelings. They're supposed to be strong, and if they break down once in a blue moon, the poor men feel they need to apologize! Women are lucky in this department. Men expect us to act like blubbering fools in a variety of situations.

The biggest challenge (as one of the volunteers agreed) is feeling comfortable with being <u>vulnerable</u>. That's it — I said it. Being vulnerable is allowing yourself to be raw, exposed, and giving your partner the chance to see that rare side of you.

When you've mastered this feat, you've conquered something not everyone is capable of doing, and your relationship will be that much stronger.

Chapter Review.

Myra bought tickets to a comedy show and asked Fred to go with her. He said he had other plans that night, so she brought her friend instead. After the show, they grabbed a cup of coffee and chatted. Myra talked about how she loved Fred, but she wished he would spend more time with her. Her friend looked Myra in the eyes and proceeded to tell Myra that Fred is just using her, and doesn't feel the same about her. "I don't want you to waste any more time or see you get hurt, move on," she urged. Myra didn't agree, explaining, "You haven't met Fred or seen us together. When you do, you will see things differently." Her friend then made a valid point, "Sweetie, if I haven't met him after six months, who knows if I ever will?"

On Valentine's Day, Fred said he had to work late, but would come over after work. At midnight, inebriated Fred showed up banging on Myra's door. She opened the door slightly and told Fred to leave. Shocked, Fred mumbled how much he missed her and wanted to see her.

Myra informed him that he hurt her feelings and she was sick of caring for someone that did not care about her. "But I do care," Fred said, as he struggled to stand up straight. "Just come in Fred, but I'm still mad at you," Myra said. Fred sweet-talked her to the bedroom and pulled a card out of his jacket pocket.

It was a funny Valentine card. Not at all romantic—just funny. "See, I didn't forget you, baby." Myra took out a box of heart chocolates and a card and handed it to him. Fred opened the card and said, "Nice babe, now let's go to bed." "Did you not see how the card says I love you Fred!" Myra stated. He replied, "You know me. I'm not made that way, how do I respond to that?" "Hmm, maybe you can say you love me too," said Myra. Fred responded with, "The best I can do is say that I do have some feelings for you and I can try to see only you, try this couple's thing out." "That's the best Valentine's Day present you could have given me Fred," she replied as she took his hand and lead him to bed.

Lanie and Bob had a great visit at Bob's parent's house. She fit right in with his family. Bob's parents really liked her as he knew they would. Lanie had been working a lot since they returned from the trip, and didn't have a lot of extra time for Bob. This started to cause some tension in the relationship because he didn't tell her how he felt and instead acted a bit distant at times. After the second time this happened, she asked him if everything was alright. He replied, "Yep," but Lanie felt he was holding back. She asked him what was wrong. "I feel like I don't see you anymore. You work so much and there isn't any time left for me." Lanie replied, "I have been under a lot of pressure at my job lately, Bob, but please know that you're very important to me."

"As soon as I finish with this account I will be able to spend more time with you. At times my work will demand a lot of me, but that doesn't mean I've forgotten you. I'm still here and I want you to always be able to talk to me about anything, anytime." Bob answered, "Yes, I understand, and I'll work on talking to you about what's wrong, instead of keeping my feelings to myself and resenting the time you devote to your job, which I know is a priority." "I guess at the beginning of the relationship I got to see so much of you that I was spoiled a bit, because I love being with you," he then went on to say. "I love being with you too," Lanie replied. "How about tonight I make you dinner and give you a long back rub?" "That sounds like a great plan," he replied with a smile.

So, when the time is right, you'll start to open up your heart, bare your soul, and come to a deeper level in your relationship.

Explore one another and cherish even the simplest moments shared, because these are some of the fondest memories you will remember.

CHAPTER SEVEN

Be Still My Beating Heart

This saying originally meant, "An expression of excitement when seeing the object of one's romantic affections," and was initially used with the swooning earnestness of woman's poetry during the Romantic period. Now, it's more often used ironically about suitors who are indisputably unsuitable. Boy, how things have changed.

In chapter seven, we explore love at first sight, how you know when you're in love, and romance.

Love is such a mystery. It makes people laugh and cry. There are many great novels, poems, and songs written about it, and people go to the edges of the earth to find it or avoid it.

Do you believe in love at first sight? I do. The stories of true love at first sight are few and far between, but I believe. Most people I questioned didn't feel the same. Also, as so many of the volunteers have proclaimed, I agree with them in the idea of "lust" at first sight. Only 31% of those questioned believe love at first sight exists, and to my amazement, slightly more men believe this than women! Vandre (23) feels it is definitely possible. Mario has not experienced it thus far, but also feels it is possible. Such positive outlooks on life. I love it!

For those of you who do believe in love at first sight, a study was done by the Rowett Research Institute at the University at Aberdeen, Scotland, to shed some light on the topic. Researchers found assortative mating occurs in "love at first sight," which means that people tend to select a mate based on physical appearance, including body fatness, social symmetry, and qualities like similar social, financial, and educational backgrounds. Pheromones are scent markers that appear in human sweat, and dictate sexual behavior. They play a large part in attraction as well.

Stephanie Ortigue, assistant professor of psychology and neurology at Syracuse University and her colleagues performed a study called "The Neurology of Love." They found that in as early as 0.2 seconds of visual contact, twelve areas of the brain work together to release many hormones and chemicals that induce the feeling of love.

I'm sure some of you have heard a story about someone who met their spouse for the first time and felt a strong innate feeling toward them. They knew they were going to spend the rest of their life with the person, despite only having just met. One of my favorite college professors had such an experience. She met her husband and he proposed within twenty-four hours. She accepted and two weeks later they were married. When I met her, she had already been married eight or nine years.

There are some who still hang onto the notion of a fairytale love. This can become an issue, because even though Disney's worth continues to climb as they churn out a new fairy tale every few years, life isn't like that. We certainly never see the castle the prince lives in foreclosed, or the future princess falling in love with his best friend instead. Things like that happen in reality.

Real love also happens, but it's seldom as easy as in the movies. When the tough times come knocking, couples have to find the will to fight that much harder for their relationship. Be realistic about love, and some days will indeed feel like a fairy tale. However, no relationship is a fairy tale every day.

Love is the best feeling in the world. It warms you inside and radiates on the outside.

I know I'm in love when I long to be with the person I love. Space is great and an essential component in the relationship, but as years go by, if I'm still excited to talk to or see the person I love and it is hard to imagine my life without him, I know I'm hooked.

It is the cherry on top of my very large sundae. It is complimentary, not supplementary. Of course, the beginning of the relationship is exciting, especially in that initial six months when you're both on your best behavior and getting to know one another. The future seems utterly hopeful and everything feels wonderful, but to me, the best part in a relationship is when you moved way past that period. You're ready for the long haul and want to be there to fully support one another. When you experience life, real problems, and unity remains, you know your love is real. There's a satisfaction in respecting each other's differences and embracing your common ground. Romantic gestures may or may not appear as often, but what they symbolize is what it's all about. I believe in telling those whom you love that you love them as much as you can, for you never know what tomorrow may bring. It is imperative to watch what flies out of your mouth when you don't see eye to eye (and let's face it, everybody has disagreements at times) because once it's out there, it's too late—you can't take it back. Your partner may forgive, but they will remember what was said. This is something I live by because life is short. I haven't always been so good or patient. Years ago, I got into arguments where I was too concerned with getting the last word or one-upping my spouse. I was so caught up in the moment that I lost track of what was important: love, respect, and the preservation of the relationship. That was another lesson I took away from my marriage. I can say that even when I've been upset with someone in future serious relationships, I have refrained from hitting below the belt. Saying something terrible out of anger or pain, may feel good in the moment, but afterwards you both suffer.

For those of you who have never been in love, you are missing out on one of life's greatest gifts. The feeling is like no other and isn't something you want to miss. Having someone in your corner can bring you back from a crazy day with a simple smile.

So how do you know when you're in love?

In 1986 the triangle theory of love was developed by Robert J. Sternberg, a psychologist at Tufts University. He proposed that true love must consist of three components that form a triangle:

1. Intimacy: The feeling of closeness, trust, bonding, connectedness, and friendship in the relationship.
2. Passion: The feeling of excitement or energy; physical attraction, romance, and arousal in the relationship.
3. Commitment: The decision to love someone and maintain loyalty to preserve the relationship.

Although relationships will change over time, becoming more or less passionate, just like the ebbs and flows of life, a combination of these three components need to be present to achieve that ideal relationship or true love. He found that with consummate love, these couples continued to share a deep desire to be with one another, even after many years.

He stresses the importance for couples to put all three components of love into action because maintaining it is a lot harder than falling in love, warning, "Even the greatest of loves can die."

Here are several of the wonderful responses received about what made people realize they were in love.

> ***Some replies from male volunteers about how they knew they were in love:***
>
> "When all I want to do is see her, be around her, and I get butterflies in my tummy."
>
> "Just a feeling you have."

"When I only want to be with that person and it has been a significant amount of time together."

"The best attempt at a description would be that you put the needs and wants of the other person above your own. You have tremendous respect and affection for the other person. You see the other person as 'completing you.' You are not dependent upon the other person, but you work together in harmony as an interdependent unit. It's the most amazing feeling in the world and you know when you are there."

"When you would do anything for that person, even give your life. You don't want to be with anyone but that person."

"Love is a choice and you will know when you sense a feeling toward that person like no other."

"If I regularly catch myself thinking of someone when I'm not busy with my regular activities, and she is the first person to come to mind when I want to hang out and I start dreaming about her, then I'd say I'm in love."

"I suppose it would be when I wake up thinking about her, and when thinking about her makes a sour day go by faster."

"When it's more important to you what the person you love wants than what you want—of course, you have to love yourself as well. It's a balancing act, a constant one—a lot of work, isn't it?"

Here are answers from the women questioned about love:

"When I have a genuine desire to put that person's needs and wants before my own. When after serious contemplation, I believe I could share my life with that person."

"When normalcy begins to regulate the relationship more than the initial butterflies you had when you first met, and you still respect and appreciate them for who they are, who they aren't, and who they can be."

"You realize you would do anything for that person without question. You feel love, companionship, protection, understanding, passion, drive, soul ties, and an intense desire to never want to live a day without sharing it with that person."

"I can't imagine my life without them."

"When you order the same entrée at dinner." (I loved that answer.)

"Anticipation, euphoria, silliness, and a warm feeling when the person is near."

"You just know. You want to be better as a person. You don't want to be with anyone but your one, and you want them to be happy. You respect them, are influenced by them; you allow your life to teach you."

"You don't stop thinking about that person for one second. You smile just knowing he's there with you or will be there with you. You look at the world in a different way because of that person. Your heart literally hurts if anything happens to him; even if nothing happens to him, but to the relationship."

Rachel explained it like this, "When the words 'I love you' accidently slip out to the person you've been seeing, it's when you realize you would take a bullet for this person without thinking twice."

Pure expressions of love contain so much hope and anticipation of the good to come. People want to feel love, share their life, hopes, dreams, and future. They need to be desired and taken care of by someone they can rely on.

"People crave understanding, touch, arousal, stimulation, drive, and passion from their other half to feel complete. All those feelings and sensations you can't complete on your own," Jessica said.

Elizabeth feels most people want to be known, saying, "We go through our entire life often unnoticed by the world we live in, but if one can identify with just one other individual, it gives you a sense of meaning and purpose. There is an unquestionable comfort derived from understanding just one other person emotionally, physically, mentally, and spiritually." I enjoyed her answer, which was filled with so much depth.

Mark (52) thinks it's having someone who cares about your welfare, a partner in life or, "You and me against the world." Powerful.

"Friendship, attention, an ego boost, romance, a kindred soul, and company," Gabriel said.

Other people mentioned respect, trust, acceptance, understanding, loyalty, similarities, steadiness, and companionship.

Timing is also an essential component when it comes to relationships. Like two ships passing in the night, people's paths can end up crossing, sometimes more than once, but it must be the right time for both for a relationship to bud and then blossom. You hear those stories where a couple met in high school or college, went on to live their lives, eventually marry, then divorce, only to cross paths many years later and rekindle what they were not ready for at the time.

Romantic gestures that go a long way.

So, let's talk about romance. I realize there are a lot of people who feel romance is corny or just plain silly, and that it should be saved for chick flicks that make girls and women believe there are men out there anxiously waiting to sweep them off their feet.

I have a book, *Everything Romantic,* which is loaded with romantic ideas and places to visit. Your imagination can easily wander, as you imagine some of the destinations such as Turtle Island in Fiji where they only allow fourteen couples on the island at one time, and announce cocktails and dinner by having musicians stroll by your bungalow serenading the guests! My favorite romantic destination I have visited during my travels thus far is Paris, France. The city just screams romance! The architecture, the lights, the cafes, and the mysterious, dimly-lit cobblestone streets. Another amazing site is Positano, Italy, on the Amalfi coast. It's breathtaking as you wind down the narrow mountain roads and see the colorful houses, quaint restaurants, shops, and the blue waters of the Tyrrhenian Sea. Another gem is Hawaii, with plush, tropical and gorgeous beaches abound. It's a very popular destination for honeymooners—you will see them toasting with their pineapple cocktails, which contain brightly colored umbrellas.

So, what does romance mean to you? Everyone will have a different answer. I think one general pick would have to be flowers. Flowers, especially roses, are at the top of the romance list. Florists make a killing on Valentine's Day, and even a romantically naive man knows if he is in trouble, a flower delivery will help ease the pain, just like ibuprofen. There are countless songs on the radio written about love and heartbreak, and I'm sure certain ones make you remember special moments in your relationships.

When you find yourself thinking of sweet gestures you can do for the one you love, that's romance at its finest.

Is romance important to a relationship?

Half of the men questioned and all the women thought romance is important in keeping a relationship fresh and alive.

"Taking each other for granted is one of the biggest causes for breakups," Mark said, and I agree. I have written, "Never take each other for granted" in wedding cards time and time again. Plan special dates, notice the little things your partner does, support them like no other, and always treat them with an utmost level of respect. Sometimes we can treat a stranger with a higher level of respect than the person we share our bed and heart with.

Raul (40) gave a girlfriend a teddy bear, a rose, created a drawing for her, and wrote her a poem. Now, that's romantic!

Vandre said, "One time the company I used to work for sent me to Norway, where I met a girl from Poland who went to New York two days after we met. A couple of weeks later I flew to New York to meet her one last time." The spontaneity he displayed even if the relationship was short-lived was priceless.

Eddie is a true romantic at heart, having written poetry and handmade Valentine cards for his mate.

Romance to Okon is cooking for his dates, which he enjoys.

Sonia (38) bought a boyfriend all new bedding, candles, flowers, wine, and had someone set it all up for her when they were out in the city for the evening. Talk about planning.

It's truly about the thought, and not the amount of money spent. Simple, creative gestures from the heart are just as special as any gesture which costs a lot of money.

Missy (29) said she bought a boyfriend some of his favorite style shirts, hid them around the house and made raunchy Post-it notes that explained where to find them.

I once sent an ex on a romantic "treasure hunt" around town. It started at the liquor store, where he had to pick up a bottle of wine, to the florist to pick up a single red rose, with instructions to meet at the restaurant where I was waiting.

Christi surprised her man with a surprise birthday cruise.

Donna had a house full of candles, soft music, rose petals on the bed, and a bubble bath waiting.

On the other hand, Lauren feels that walking through a city in the rain (without an umbrella) or sneaking away to the top of a mountain in the middle of the night spells romance. Invigorating!

Someone I once dated showed up at my job in a borrowed Rolls Royce with a dozen roses. Another sent a singing pink gorilla with a balloon bouquet, filled my apartment with cards and flowers, hid a square box with a big red bow in the car, and finally surprised me with a night at the theatre. I felt really special. There have been moonlit walks in the rain, surprise dinners that took all day to cook, breakfast in bed, homemade cards, poems, and lots of other wonderfully grand and delightful simple gestures.

Chapter Review.

Fred and Myra spent a good amount of time together for a few weeks (after Fred agreed to try to commit to Myra) and even made it out in public twice. The next few months offered more of the same. Fred started seeing other women again and calling Myra less. She often called to question what was going on. He said he was busy at work. Myra found herself leaving angry messages on his voicemail and she even showed up at his apartment late one evening, pounding on his door when she saw two cars in his driveway, and only the bedroom light on. Fred never came to the door and Myra went home in tears.

The next day Fred finally answered her call and told her one of the guys crashed at his place because he had drunk too much. Myra said she didn't believe him. Fred said he tried the couple's thing out, but it was too hard.

"So I see other girls, but you're the one I think about most often." "I should be all you need, we have been together ten months!" Myra exclaimed. Fred answered with, "Cut me some slack, I have a lot going on. Don't pressure me."

"It's only because I love you that I'm sticking around waiting for you to grow up Fred," Myra said.

"I have to go, Myra, my boss is calling me," Fred replied.

Bob and Lanie have been doing well. Both of them joined the gym and work out together. They went on a camping trip with two other couples and took a painting class one Saturday, which they enjoyed. The two spend two to three nights a week together. They do little things to make each other happy. When Bob sleeps over, Lanie always makes him a mean cup of coffee after they awaken, and he massages her feet after a hard day of work. Bob is always cleaning out her drain when she clogs it with her long locks of hair, and Lanie makes his favorite comforting meal, a meat loaf whenever he craves it. They've also been adjusting to their differences. Lanie got irritated whenever Bob threw his bath towel on her floor, never quite making it to the hamper, and it drove him crazy when she turns on all the lights in his house, then forgets to turn them off.

Bob has strong political views, whereas Lanie barely votes, which at first had him questioning her patriotism. She loves to stay up late and watch movies, but Bob likes to read in bed and go to sleep early. Did they try to change one another? Call each other names and say the way they do things or what they believe is wrong? No. They learned to embrace their differences, compromise, communicate whatever bothers them, and respect their partner's views. Relationships come with bumps in the road—that's inevitable. It's the way you smooth out the bumps that counts.

Romance is not all about flowers, expensive presents, lavish endeavors or candlelit dinners. It can be anything from a simple love note left on your mirror after your loved one has left for work, to a massage at the end of a long day. It is someone who stands by your side when you wake up in a hospital room or dances with you in the middle of your living room. It can be the pillow fight you had last Tuesday, or a quiet moment between you when there aren't any questions that need to be asked, no words to be said, because you know what the other is thinking. The perfect moment can be simple and profound, like gazing at your baby together moments after he or she was born. These are the experiences that define romance. These are the moments that take your breath away.

CHAPTER EIGHT

Active Daters Verses Hoppers

Are you serious about finding "the one?" An active dater is someone who actually goes out on dates, not just "hangs out" with someone and may be searching for that special someone, dating different people. They may not be looking for anything serious at the present time, but enjoy dating and meeting new people. Of course, not everyone enjoys dating. There are active daters who wish they could find that special person because they're tired of dating, but they feel good enough about themselves to be alone, because they have created interesting, or hopefully sensational single lives.

The hopper is someone who can never be alone. Alone to them is scarier than their first horror film that gave them nightmares for a week. The hopper will always have a partner, but when they begin to tire of their current mate, they'll search for a replacement while still in the present relationship. I call them hoppers because they literally hop from one relationship to another, with no alone time in between. They will stay with their current partner even if they are miserable. The devil they know still feels a bit more warm and fuzzy compared to the mystery of the unknown. As soon as a new "angel" crosses their path, they will hop like a bunny with all their bunny baggage right into their arms.

In this chapter, we explore active daters and hoppers, and you will soon find out which group you fall into.

There are those who continually meet the current Mr. or Ms. Right within a month of their last relationship. Others look at them and think they're lucky. Falling into a new relationship shortly after the old one ends isn't as rosy as they make it seem. Hoppers like to overlook the obvious because the need to fulfill the mission of being in a relationship is stronger than waiting until someone more suitable comes along. They need to be in a relationship, and are good at convincing themselves that their last boyfriend or girlfriend wasn't the one for them, and is now a distant memory. This new person, however, is for sure, "The One."

Loneliness, low self-worth, and not wanting to be without sex for any extended period of time (especially for men) are all strong predictors here.

Convenience isn't the only motivator for hoppers. Fear also plays a big part in their relationships, and for a lot of people. We're all plagued by doubt. Negative thoughts start creeping in. What if I never meet someone I'm crazy about? What if I end up alone? Everyone will think I have a problem because I've never been married, or I must find someone because all my friends are married, and my pool of singles friends is now obsolete! Recently, someone I know said to me, "What if I don't find someone I like better? And I end up alone? It's hard to meet nice girls and she is a great person." He'd just got out of a relationship. My reply was quick and certain: "When you meet the right person you can't live without, you'll know it. It's hard to explain, but you'll just know. Until then, don't settle. If you do end up staying single, is that so bad? You simply will have to make sure you live the best single life possible."

Some people choose to remain single and are proud of it. A portion of this group doesn't want to get married because the divorce rate is 50%, or they may not want to have to bend to meet someone else's needs. Also, some worry about the lack of variety, and fear they're not going to be satisfied with one person, like eating the same cereal every day. Others enjoy having long-term relationships, but they simply chose not to walk down the aisle. They feel a piece of paper does not define devotion. Famous people like Oprah, Al Pacino, John Hamm and Charlize Theron have always been very open about not wanting to get married. Although like Oprah, they can be happy being with only one mate, and sometimes these relationships can last longer than some marriages.

People who truly have a fear of commitment frequently come from homes where they watched parents in a troubled relationship that ended in divorce. Traumatic backgrounds only exacerbate this. Parents that were either under-involved or over-involved to the point of enmeshment often produce children that struggle in relationships.

In 2011, the Pew Research Center released data showing that barely half of U.S. adults are married, the lowest percentage ever. In 1960, 72% of U.S. adults ages eighteen and older were married, compared with 51% today. The most dramatic decline in marriage occurred among the ages eighteen to twenty-nine, where 20% today are married, versus 59% in 1960.

Which category do you find yourself in? Do you hop like the Easter bunny from relationship to relationship, or are you taking your time in choosing a mate?

While hoppers have their problems, active daters aren't immune from bumps in the road either.

Active dating can feel like a part-time job if you let it. Try to keep it light and have as much fun as possible. Try not to think of it as a chore, but an exciting way to meet new, interesting people. You have to keep plugging along and continue the search, though I do realize sometimes it can be daunting. I once took a hiatus from dating after being single for a long while, because dating was starting to become another "to-do" on my list, instead of simply enjoying myself and having fun. I joked that even if Mr. Right came along I wouldn't look twice, because I was taking a break for a few months. Since then I have taken many needed breaks, mini-dating halts, and I'm not thinking of dating as some mission that needs to be fulfilled.

Try your very best to be true to yourself as well as to others, by not getting into situations where you're second fiddle. You never want to be waiting in the wings for the person you're dating to squeeze you into their busy schedule. Wait for someone who thinks you're the most amazing person they've met in quite some time. If the person you're dating is not able to make time for you at least once a week, they have something or someone else on their agenda. There will be times when one of you will have so much on your plate that you may skip a week, but if this happens consistently, then man's furry best friend can give you more attention, and you should graciously exit the relationship.

"Change" is the one constant that you can always count on.

As we have discussed, dating has changed over time. It's all too common for two people to meet, hang out once, have fun between the sheets, and continue "hanging out," but never really go anywhere. The girls usually think this is a relationship, but guys think otherwise. I'm not blaming the guys, because traditional dating is such a foreign concept to many. Men know better but figure, why bother or do all the work when I can get away with doing nothing? As per our discussion on nude pictures and Netflix and Chill — it's too easy. Women also play a part in relaxing these standards.

It saddens me because many young people today are desperately trying to be seen and heard, crying out for help, and they will do anything, not necessarily for love, but to simply have someone like them. It isn't only young people searching for love in all the wrong places. People fill that void within their soul with drugs, food, self-mutilation, gambling, sex or whatever it takes to simply FEEL, or to temporarily ease their pain. When you feel so bad and don't know how to make the pain go away, you spiral out of control and don't know how to get back on your feet. Everyone has a story, but some have to hit rock bottom before realizing they've been ignoring their deepest, inner feelings. Others learn from life experiences and then finally demand something better because life is too brief to waste. One of my favorite sayings is: "It's not a dress rehearsal, live the life you've imagined!" — Thoreau.

Do you think most people prefer to play the field (variety is the spice of life), or are they searching for that special someone?

From my work, I believe a large amount of people are definitely searching.

A few responses showed that there is a time in life where playing the field is more appropriate, and, let's face it — many of us have been there and some chose to remain there permanently. After my divorce, I didn't want a serious relationship for three years, and had a wonderful journey exploring where I wanted to go and what I wanted to do with my life. I celebrated myself and my single life.

Do we want one person? Or do we want many?
David (35) said, "The answer to this question is 'both.' We want a girl we love that we do everything with, including sex, and other girls to have sex with. Just like food. We want to eat dinner with the girl we love often, but we also want to eat with our friends, by ourselves, masturbation, etcetera. It's just biology."

Mickey (22) wrote, "Somewhere in between."

Mark stated that when he was younger he played the field, but feels it should only be a phase.

And Jerry (69) said, "One person at a time, unless she's a twin." Good one, Jerry.

Missy says, "Right now I would like to figure out one person."

Elizabeth feels playing the field is overrated. "I would prefer to get to know one individual and know that I can trust them, without fear of them deciding to 'spice up' their life behind my back."

Sonia (38) feels, "Definitely one person at a time."

What I found interesting is that people of all ages have one thing in common. The majority (77%) of women and men are looking for that special someone to make everything seem right. Thirteen percent prefer to play the field, 6% felt they would only be faithful to one person the day they decided to walk down the aisle, and 4% said it depends where they were in their life at the time.

As human beings, we all crave companionship. There's something comforting in knowing we're all looking for the same thing.

Let's catch up with our two couples:

Chapter Review.

Fred continued to sweet talk Myra to let him come over after he went out with the guys (or other women) about once a week, sometimes more often and sometimes less. He would invite Myra over on Monday nights (his down day where he never went out), and always begged her to cook for the two of them. She tried to get him to engage in deep conversation with her, or any conversation for that matter, but Fred was satisfied with flipping channels on the remote, and only paid attention to the TV. He only seemed to notice she was there when he wanted to hit the bedroom, or sofa, or wherever he wanted to get naked.

This continued to bother Myra, but she felt she couldn't do any better than Fred. Who would want her? She thought it was better than being alone.

Things got worse. Monday came and went without a call from Fred. Myra called him, but he didn't return the call. Then Tuesday, Wednesday and Thursday came, and there wasn't a peep from him, which greatly concerned her. The weekend arrived, she called and texted Fred frantically, then drove by his house. He wasn't there. She went home and drowned her tears in a tub of chocolate ice cream. She continued to send him many messages and woke up early on Sunday (let's face it, she didn't sleep well anyway), doing yet another drive by his place which bordered on stalking. As the days passed Myra continued to try to reach him with no success. Fred disappeared like batteries during hurricane season. The next weekend was quickly approaching and Myra was angry and depressed. She felt she was expending too much energy in a relationship with someone who simply did not give a damn. Finally, on Saturday she knocked on Fred's door, and he answered. He invited her in and Myra questioned him. "Where have you been and why have you been avoiding me?"

"I've met someone else. It just happened and I didn't know what to say," he answered.

Myra felt the tears coming but held them back and yelled instead, "Seriously? I've spent over a year with you, putting up with all of your shenanigans, and this is what I get?"

"It just happened!" he yelled.

"Nothing just happens, Fred," Myra cried.

"Hey, I'm sorry, but did you really think we had something Myra?" he said. "Hanging out with you was cool, but come on! I'm just keeping it real," Fred stated.

"I'm so done! Fine, it's over. I hope you're miserable together," Myra cried, as she ran out the door and slammed it behind her.

Lanie's birthday was around the corner and Bob had a fun surprise party planned for her with all their closest friends and family. He was going to transform his yard into an "old Hollywood movies" theme party due to her love of classic movies.

Bob and Lanie's sisters made the props. He borrowed an old projector so he can flash cute and embarrassing pictures of his love through the years. He sent out the invitations, and he, along with family and friends would be doing all the cooking. As the date approached he was a bit anxious that Lanie may find out about the surprise. A week before, he informed her that he was going to make her a special dinner for her birthday. She flashed Bob a big smile, kissed him, and told him how nice that would be. On Lanie's birthday Bob worked all day to make it as special as possible. Those closest to her helped to make the day extraordinary.

He picked her up and drove to his house. Everyone parked a few blocks away to hide their cars. Bob opened the door and led Lanie through the house toward the door, which opened to the backyard. He stood in front of the door as Lanie asked, "Did you make me a romantic dinner under the stars, sweetie?" Bob opened the door

> and everyone yelled, "Surprise!" Lanie was shocked, but obviously delighted. Friends and family hugged her and wished her a happy birthday. She looked at Bob, laughed, and said, "I can't believe you were able to hide this from me, you're so bad at keeping a secret! Thank you so much, honey. You know how much I love old movies and I love all the decorations! Everyone did a great job making the yard look amazing, especially you!" She put her arms around his neck, kissed him and enjoyed her memorable birthday.

Persistence pays.

To those of you who are dating and enjoying yourselves: embrace this period in your life. Women, plan that perfect outfit, and men, come up with an idea for a fabulous date as both anxiously wait to see one another. You can also be proud for taking the plunge again and again, when at times you may feel like you're unable to go on one more date! You're putting yourself out there and you won't settle. You have to realize it may take quite some time to find someone you really connect with, but isn't it worth the wait? Enjoy being single and remember — the single life can be fun. Enjoy all the benefits that come along with it in the meantime. You have more time to spend with friends or to take that class you've been excited about. You can eat cereal for dinner, watch chick flicks or sports, and not have to share the remote! You can do what you want, when you want, without having to tell anyone what you've been doing all day. You get to meet new people, check out new hot spots or simply visit your favorite hang-outs. You can sleep late and sprawl all over the bed you have all to yourself. You can go on that vacation with family or friends, and focus on your career or that business you've been dying to start. The only problems you must address are ones that directly affect you, and as you engage in a drama/stress-free life as much as possible, they'll be very limited. However you choose to spend your spare time, celebrate your remarkable single self every day because you're worth it!

A word to hoppers: Stop hopping or you may end up down the rabbit hole.
If you slow down long enough and look inside yourself, you just might figure out what you've been running from. Allow yourself even a short period of time alone, you might appreciate the wonderful person you are, without having another person by your side.

At the end of the day, you should decide the best course of action for you, because this is your one and only fabulous life! ***Laissez faire!***

CHAPTER NINE

Is it a Bump in the Road or a Boulder?

"When it is dark enough you can see the stars."
—Ralph Waldo Emerson,
American Essayist, Poet, and Philosopher,
c. 1803–1882.

I remember a time when I looked into the eyes of someone and couldn't even imagine what we would ever fight about, because we always seemed to see eye to eye. Well, one day it happened. We had our first argument. When that happens, you fall off that little cloud you've been riding on and then reality hits you. To think you're never going to disagree is just plain silly.

Chapter Nine will be examining bumps and boulders, the warning signs that alert us to when it's time to get out and the issues that may arise, or when a potential or current partner may turn dangerous.

Disagreement done in a way that still shows you respect your partner is healthy. If you walk around on egg shells, scared that you'll rock the boat or upset your partner with your opposing view, that's not healthy for either one of you. Is that how you really want to live? You never want to sacrifice who you are for someone else and become a carbon copy. The person you're dating should respect the fact you have your own opinion, as you will do the same.

"They never said it was going to be easy." I love this saying. Relationships can be messy; they are a lot of work, but the rewards are well worth it. Love is a "verb," and yes, it requires action.

But what if your relationship isn't worth it? When do you call it quits?

I feel there are two opposite extremes in relationships that are prevalent. The pool of people that are happy in their relationships and stay together for the long haul are dwindling. This phenomenon has been occurring for decades. People are either hanging onto relationships that are clearly not good for them so they won't be alone, or the opposite occurs—they decide to get married, give it a try and run at the first sign of trouble. Remember the statistic we learned earlier. The researchers concluded that less than 5% make it to the "complete acceptance" stage in relationships.

Not every relationship is meant for a happily ever after; sometimes it's better to break up than prolong the misery. How do you know when it's time?

If you're asking this question, it might very well be time.

In my opinion, some people tend to hold on far longer than they should when they know the relationship is hopeless.

They wait until someone else comes along because they don't enjoy their own company, or they feel bad, because, let's face it, breaking up isn't easy, no matter how many times you do it. I have experimented with different ways to approach breaking up and unless you are on the same page and not happy with the way things are going, their reaction can be rather unpleasant. Or in some cases, downright shocking.

Hanging on when things have been stale for a long time and you have both become complacent isn't healthy either. When you commit to someone, you agree to not see anyone else, and if you're married, you'll be committed to that person for as long as you live. If you can recognize when a form of "renewal" needs to happen in your relationship, hopefully you will both be able to keep the relationship fresh when it starts getting stale. Couples need to pay attention to this and work to do different things to avoid years of the same old mundane routine. Ever see a couple in a restaurant who remain completely silent throughout their entire meal, with little eye contact? Very sad. Feeling comfortable enough with a person to feel content with pure silence while together is fine. There have been moments in my life where mutual silence was blissful, but when you're not saying a peep to one another in a busy restaurant in an hour or more and there aren't any hands being held, no eye contact or open lines of communication, it's not good.

Non-verbal communication is more telling than people think. Watch people interact at a mall or an airport and you'll learn a lot. Sometimes you can be so attracted to a person, your thought process gets a bit jaded — until one day you look at them and wonder how you stayed together as long as you did, because you are from two completely different worlds.

One major problem with marriages today, is it's way too easy to get divorced. I know because I got divorced. I never thought when walking down the aisle that my marriage would end in a dissolution document. Initially, the stigma attached to the word bothered me a lot, especially at such a young age.

There are some couples who try out marriage, and when it doesn't seem to be working after a few disagreements in the first year of marriage, they simply walk away, stating, "We gave it a try and it didn't work, oh well." It's just too easy. You can even buy a do-it-yourself kit. I've even heard of a drive-through divorce! If more people took the time and effort into breaking down what they're doing wrong and work toward implementing change, they could build a stronger, healthier marital unit, and there would be fewer divorces. Why change or look at yourself and what may need to be worked on, when you can flirt with someone new and possibly repeat the same dance over again? People generally aren't quick to admit fault and instantaneously blame the other person, but if they were so bad, how did you end up with them in the first place? You once loved one another, remember?

Trouble around the corner.

Everybody loves attention and wants to be wanted. Some take this to a different level by craving it so much, they end up sabotaging the good thing they already have.

Others try too hard. Have you ever met someone who wanted to be in a relationship so badly that they give too much and appear desperate? As much as you may want to, you can't make a relationship happen overnight. Relationships need to blossom like a flower, and that takes time. You can skip through the steps and run out and have a shotgun wedding, but how many of those do you know are still together?

Showing you're interested is important, but when the person you just started dating talks about moving in with you, and you are yet to know their middle name, it's a problem.

When someone you're interested in is doting all over you, it's flattering, as long as they're not too needy. Being needy is not flattering. It's a sign of insecurity in a relationship.

Finding a happy medium.

The key to dating, and in life for that matter is "everything in moderation," which is a simple guide to live by. A happy medium strives for genuineness, quality and intimacy in relationships. You want it to be more than mediocre but also wish to avoid craziness and drama. Obviously, your goal should be to thrive in a relationship, but if you've tried and tried again and failed, you need to really think about whether you should keep trying. You do whatever it takes to make it work (because something inside you says it's truly worth it), or you walk away — for the right reasons. Only you will know that answer, and if you decide to stay, your other half must want it just as much as you do.

"Be brave and fight for it, or be strong enough to walk away and stand alone."

Dating is practice for marriage, if and when someone ever decides they want to make that commitment. If the person you're dating clearly can't communicate, has drama as their middle name, or constantly keeps you guessing about how they feel, it might be time for you to move on to greener pastures.

There are individuals who are emotionally unavailable and believe they want a relationship, but when things start to get more serious, erratic behavior ensues. They're incapable of true intimacy due to many reasons. It may not ever be possible for them, but it's up to them to work on whatever is holding them back. You will not get them to magically transform into the woman or man you wish they can become.

If you can communicate positively when you're dating, and learn to fight fair, you're one step ahead of the game. If you can talk about anything, anytime, and listen to what your partner has to say without raising your voice when you disagree, you'll be a gem who will be sought after.

One problem I see repetitively while working with couples; the man feels he is pulling his weight in the relationship because he goes to work every day and provides for his girlfriend or wife, and shows her how much he cares by taking her out. If they cohabitate, he demonstrates this by paying bills, etcetera. On the other hand, the woman is upset because she wants him to buy her flowers, help her around the house, or tell her how nice she looks. A lot of the time, she also works full-time and does most of the household duties, and is more involved with child rearing.

The man tells me if she feels this way, she should just ask him to help and do these things for her, because he's not a "mind reader." The woman tells me she shouldn't have to "tell him." He should know how she feels, realize what needs to be done and just do it. She goes on to say that when he does do these things without her pushing him into it, he wants to be praised, whereas she does these things all day long and isn't hearing constant praise. I explain to them that neither viewpoint is wrong; men and women communicate differently, and if they want to have a harmonious relationship, they should work with instead of against their differing communication styles and life will be easier.

I know women and men who have placed all members of the opposite sex into a "no good" pool, as if they are good for nothing. They have been scorned or previous partners have treated them badly, and they hold onto so much anger. My advice is to let it go, just let it go. Walking around with anger is truly bad for your health, and you're sending out negative vibes to any potential love interests.

Has someone ever given you signs they were clearly unhappy but you refused to acknowledge them, hoping these signs would soon disappear?

The writing is on the wall, but you just aren't reading it? One quarter of those I asked have experienced this. The small percentage of people who admit to this happening were mainly women. At times, people just want someone so badly, they try to pretend things are not as bad as they really are, because they're trying to avoid facing the music. They refuse to walk away for whatever reason. In the passing years, I have listened to people in relationships who were simply being strung along. Their mate didn't have the courage to break up with them, so they start to engage in what I call "creative dating." They continually do everything in their power to show the person they're dating just how not into them they are, hoping their partner will get sick of the substandard treatment and end it first. First the excuses start, as the person on the short end of the stick starts trying to convince themselves everything is fine. "Maybe he's busy at work," they tell themselves, or, "Maybe she needs some space, she has been a bit stressed."

My male friends say they have purposely acted negatively to their girlfriends with the hope that they would break up with them, so they didn't have to be the one to do it. I don't know anyone that enjoys hurting someone, but life is made up of pleasantries, as well as un-pleasantries. Take a deep breath, step up to the plate, and just do it. The other person deserves to hear the truth, and hearing it sooner rather than later is preferable.

Another popular dating antic people engage in is the "fade out," which usually leads into a disappearing act. This is also known as "ghosting." Ghosting is the opposite of the types of people who string the soon-to-be ex along. The Fade Outs simply start with calling or texting less and less, answer your calls or texts less often, and eventually disappear completely.

Even more disheartening and more popular, are people who started dating someone or may have been in a relationship for quite some time, act like everything is wonderful, and then suddenly, they disappear one day as if abducted by aliens, never to be heard from again. Poof! They're gone, you've been ghosted! You wouldn't believe how often I hear this. This move, readers, is what separates the women from the girls, and the men from the boys. This dating maneuver is even worse than breaking up by text, which is also a pathetic way to break up with someone, but at least they receive some sort of closure, even if it's a cowardly way out. There is a lot of disregard for people's feelings going on today. Technology is jading people's scope of what's morally right or wrong. Years ago, you couldn't hide behind your phone or computer and take the easy way out at the expense of another's feelings. I was reading a magazine article recently and the guy writing it admitted he held on to relationships for longer than he should have, when he knew he didn't want to be in them long term. He didn't know how to end it and eventually "disappeared," because he didn't want to hurt the women's feelings, or hear them cry because it would make him "feel bad." We can say he pulled off a "combination" of the tactics. I said at the beginning of this chapter that people's reactions can be downright surprising, and I've had some less than pleasant experiences when I've told someone I no longer wanted to see them for whatever reason. Breaking up is hard, but if it truly isn't working, then I think it's the kindest thing to do. Whether you need to tell someone you have dated five times, five months or for five years that you no longer want to be with them anymore, you may not get a reaction that will be filled with joy. It's simply part of dating and being man or woman enough to take whatever they dish out, because their feelings are likely to have been hurt. I get it, guys. You hate seeing women get emotional, but it's still part of the process. In the best of situations (which I have also encountered), the person thanks you for being honest and wishes you the best. If you've encountered this and haven't figured out why your boyfriend of girlfriend refuses to return your calls, then "no answer is the answer," and unfortunately, you're dating someone who hasn't fully grown up and doesn't want to see you anymore. They're likely too scared to tell you to your face, or at the very least by phone. Hold your head up high, try not to spend another minute thinking about them and their M.I.A. status, and move on. They've done you a favor, because someone is waiting for you who will treat you the way you deserve.

Not every day is going to be sunshine and rainbows. The other person deserves honesty and to not be strung along or left wondering why you broke up with them.

One of the volunteers said, "You have got to let them decide to end their unhappiness." I feel the couple needs to communicate before it gets this far and work on their issues, or, if they're incompatible from the start, part as friends. As hard as it is, honesty is still the best policy. In any relationship, it's imperative to be able to discuss anything with one another. If you feel comfortable discussing topics with your partner that you generally feel uncomfortable talking about, it's a good sign, because your partner is listening with a caring heart and not judging you. It's also important to know when to communicate something that's bothering you. Ladies, when your boyfriend is in the middle of watching the big game he has been dying to watch all week, this isn't a good time. Also, steer away from the old "we have to talk" line, as men cringe when they hear it, and the words will automatically put some of them on defense. Stay away from leaving a voice message or text in the middle of the day previewing the talk. Just talk. When the time is right, say it from the heart and use "I" statements, expressing how <u>you feel</u> about what your partner may be doing, and then come to some sort of resolution that you <u>both</u> can agree on. Also, make sure you express how much you care about the other person because you're on the same team, which we seem to forget at times. Men, please try your best to sweeten your reaction to what your girlfriend has done to upset you, because she isn't "one of the guys." Women can be sensitive, so try using the same protocol as the ladies and get down to what <u>you</u> are <u>feeling</u>. Although it may seem like the truth, something like, "You have been acting like such a bitch lately," is not a good way to lead.

Use specific examples, and keep it about your feelings. "When you were angry at me for being late, that made me feel like you didn't understand the kind of stress I'm facing at work, and how hard I tried to get there on time." It is a fact that women are more apt to criticize, whereas men tend to stonewall (avoidance of interaction). Both parties naturally act defensively during conflict and engage in contempt (acting disrespectful), which is another form of ineffective communication, as per relationship expert, John Gottman. He also found that when you get to the core of problems, everyone wants to know: no matter what happens and no matter what I do, will you still be there for me??

I loved what Virginia (68) had to say: "I have a short attention span. The relationship would not have gotten to that point without my addressing it or ending it." Again, clear and open communication is key. In my work with couples who have been on the verge of divorce, I have witnessed them transform their relationships and gain a newfound respect for one another. They wanted their relationship to work, loved their partner, and were willing to do what it took. With an open heart and a lot of work, they established new patterns of communication, which is hard to do. We all get set in our ways and "new" can be scary. We hang on to what we know, how we interact, are used to doing things a certain way, even if it's not the healthiest way, and may end up driving two people apart. Like engaging in a dance, we'll do the same steps over and over until we decide to learn some new steps. I do believe love is a choice, and yes, a choice worth choosing.

When you start dating, a little mystery is exciting. However, do show the person that you like them. Appearing too excited to hurry up and enter into a relationship will only scare off the other person before you even get your chance at romance. Men pay very close attention to what women say and how they act, especially when the couple first starts dating. They are scared they may end up with the wrong woman, and that she may try to control everything he does once they finally settle down. Men tend to take great care in testing women to see what makes them tick (either consciously or unconsciously). A man may come on strong and then pull back. This hot and cold scenario may happen again in the future, getting close before he suddenly feels the innate urge to be alone for a bit. If a couple has engaged in this dance several times and the woman doesn't try to take control of the situation by lassoing her man, tying him down, and questioning his every motive, then they're off to a great start. Ladies, want your man to run away like a spooked horse? Stop having an independent life aside from your relationship. Your man shouldn't be your entertainment committee, nor should you be theirs. Men want to be in your life, not become your life. A friend told me recently that a man may feel like he wants a relationship one day, and then the next day feel the opposite. He said this can even fluctuate throughout the day at times. With women, biologically being more apt to focus on one man over time, with the goal of an eventual relationship, the peaks and valleys are not as sporadic. Still, uncertainty does happen to both men and women in relationships. Recently, my friend was dating someone he really liked; they went on many dates and were starting to get a bit more serious. He was letting her pace the relationship, but told her he would like to start seeing her more than once a week if she was up to it. He would work around her schedule because they both had demanding jobs and a lot of activities they enjoyed separately. One evening, they were out having what he thought was another great date. At the end of it, she told him things were moving too fast. He contacted her once since, but her reply wasn't promising.

I know a story about a man that started dating a woman he was good friends with, then realized he wasn't ready for a serious relationship and moved away. He dated other women and got into another relationship with someone else, but they continued to remain friends. Two years later he moved back, ready for a serious commitment; they started dating again, got married, and now have two children. If someone hasn't worked through all their issues from a previous relationship, if the timing isn't right or if something feels "off," you may be going along just fine then suddenly second guess the person you're with. Commitment can be overwhelming at times, and everyone is trying to get it right. Taking a break to work through your feelings is a good idea. You'll be able to see what's going on within yourself more objectively and will realize if you miss the other person when you're apart. If your partner says they need some time alone, give them the space. Try not to show them how upset you are, beg them to stay, or bombard them with questions. They will respect you tremendously and might even be quite shocked if you simply say, "Okay." If you're meant to be together, in the end, you will be.

I realize when you start dating someone new it can be very exciting, but take care to avoid pre-labeling a relationship when you're not completely sure you're in one yet. Do not act as if you are prematurely in a relationship. Also, please never try to control anyone. I feel this applies equally to people who are married as well.

A few days ago, someone told me that a happy medium is hard to find. He meets a lot of women who either just want to party all night long or want to settle down, get married, and have babies after knowing him for two weeks.

RED ALERT.

As wonderful as dating and relationships can be, it can also be dangerous. When you date, you must always be watchful.

The fact of the matter is, despite the fact there are many good people out in the world, there are unsavory characters as well. You just have to be sensible.

I have done a lot of research related to sociopaths and antisocial personality disorder, and it's more common than you think. Sociopaths have a basic lack of caring and empathy, and many of them can become violent. There's a reason why police always look at a spouse (or girlfriend/boyfriend) first when someone is murdered. There are countless shows on TV spelling out disturbing details of love gone wrong, where someone lost control and hurt or killed their loved one in an act of rage. As discussed in chapter three, when you're meeting someone for the first few dates, unless you have known them for a while or you know someone you trust that can vouch for their character, meet them at a public place until you feel comfortable enough to have them pick you up at home. Refrain from having so many cocktails that you're unable to drive. Not only will it make you appear less than desirable to your potential mate, but you're putting yourself in a compromising position. Remember, ladies, everyone said Ted Bundy (a serial killer) was a smart, attractive, "nice" guy, and the mere mention of the name Jodi Arias is sure to send chills down any man's spine. Men and women alike: you can't always trust everything your date says. People you first meet are not going to tell you that "entrepreneur" in their world really means "drug dealer." If you see a few licenses fall out of the woman you're dating's purse, and she isn't under twenty-one with a fake identification, be aware she could be a con-artist. I'm not saying you should be paranoid, waiting for your date to deceive you or to play mind tricks on you, but just be cautious until they have earned your trust. Even if you are lonely, desire a serious relationship, and enjoy the sex you may be having, be cautious until you really know the person you're with. It's easy to move them in, but moving them out can be harder.

If the person you just started seeing makes you their entire world because their life is empty, warning bells should be sounding. I'm not talking about two people that spend endless hours together because they're overjoyed in the throes of a new relationship. This one will be easy to spot if you pay attention; if they are overly intense and showing an almost obsessive interest, be careful. Trauma is one of my specialties, and I have seen and heard things you wouldn't want to imagine. I have witnessed people in relationships who can't go to the corner store without having their partner call them, because they need to check in all the time. People who are that jealous and insecure do their best and often succeed in isolating their partner from their friends and even their family.

Things can also get dangerous. Domestic violence happens to both women and men. It doesn't discriminate and affects people from all walks of life. Years ago, I was an abuse hotline counselor/volunteer at a women's resource center. I had women calling me from different places, such as under their bed and many other locations, after fleeing their homes. They were terrified and some didn't make it to the shelter I was trying to get them into, because they changed their mind and didn't show. The threat of being killed if they left echoed in their mind so loudly, they ended up going back. Imagine the terror they must have felt. Abusers will isolate their victims and tear them down so badly that they strip them of any sense of self-worth. They put their victims in a position where they rely on them financially, using threats as a tactic to keep them under their thumb. Sadly, there have been people that have escaped the terror they endured at home, only to be caught and killed. When someone acts like they are in control of you and you let them, you should think about the Mommy or Daddy issues you may have, because you're in a relationship with their replacement.

If you want to be in a relationship so badly that you'll tolerate any form of abuse, you need to look at the bigger picture, which is YOU. Doing this means working on loving yourself again and not accepting inferior treatment from anyone, because you deserve more. Please get help as soon as possible, so you can get away from this individual and be safe.

The phantom of fear: the stalker.

Have you ever encountered a stalker or a stalker-like situation? There is currently a TV show about people that have been stalked because so many have had to live through this nightmare. Anyone who has been stalked or terrorized for any extended amount of time, my heart goes out to them. I can't even imagine how horrific it must be to constantly live in fear and always have to look over your shoulder.

My friend went on two dates recently with a guy that quickly became a five-alarm clinger. After their second date, he called and kept questioning her about how she felt about him, when she would see him next, etcetera. He called again a couple of times that night (my friend had already gone to bed). She said she didn't think things would work out between them. He continued calling her many times over the next three weeks, and she ignored his calls. He finally got the message and stopped calling. Whew!

Stalkers aren't always men, either. I endured a stalking situation many years ago with a woman that wasn't happy when her ex-boyfriend had moved on. This situation was relatively short lived but was very taxing. Although it came close, the authorities didn't have to get involved, but not everyone is as lucky.

My research revealed that 17% had an experience with some sort of stalking behavior. Thankfully, no one got to the point where they needed to call the police or file a restraining order. A few people who didn't experience this said, "No! Thank God." People who have been seriously stalked for any length of time live in constant fear. They feel violated, unsure of what their stalker may do next, afraid for their lives, and some have been hurt or worse, killed by a sick or obsessed individual. If you ever have ever been put in a situation that makes you feel uneasy, or if your ex won't leave you alone no matter how many times you have asked, put an end to the behavior immediately by contacting the authorities. Your life could be on the line, so never take it lightly.

Breaking up is hard to do, but you can get over a break up.

Thankfully, the majority of break ups usually don't end in stalking. That doesn't mean breaking up is ever easy. If you can master breaking up with someone honestly with no feelings of ill will, then my hat's off to you. The pain can be devastating. Your heart aches, you may not want to go out for a little while, and for some, it takes a long time to recover. You may pour your heart out to your friends to try to lessen the pain, but you must work through the loss, and it simply takes time. You have to get reacquainted with the single you again, and face the realization that you won't be living your happily ever after with this person (if that's what you wanted). When two people go their separate ways, this is the time to re-evaluate your life. Each relationship is a learning experience. Each person has been put on our path for a reason, I truly feel nothing is an accident. Work through your baggage, even if it's just a small carry on, and take some time away from dating until you feel ready to date again. It wouldn't be fair to anyone new you meet if your heart is still pining away for your lost love.

A growth experience extraordinaire.
Essentially, you get more from less. Eventually, when someone does come into your life, you'll be a stronger partner. This can potentially be the best part of your life: full of lessons where you learn to be alone, and get to know yourself. You become more independent and realize you can not only survive, but actually thrive being on your own. It's initially a struggle, but eventually you develop other interests more fully, and recognize the joy of independence by putting more reliance on yourself. You'll probably see deeper into people, places and ideas you only treated casually before.

Taking the plunge. When will I be ready?
So many people dread starting to date again after a break up, and who can blame them? It can be challenging to start over again, but when you meet someone you adore, it's pretty amazing.

So how long should you wait? How long does it take to recover after a breakup?
Personally, I say everyone and each situation is different. It depends how you felt about this person, who broke up with whom, and many other factors. When something inside feels right, when you can say you are ready to start dating again and when you stop talking non-stop about your ex, you may be ready. People constantly say how much they can't stand their ex, but if they're talking about them that much, even if what they're saying isn't pleasant, are they really over them? There is a very fine line between love and hate. Twenty two percent of the people I questioned felt the same way I do. Every situation and every person is unique. Nineteen percent of people thought the right time was between a week and one month. Twenty four percent chose two to four months, 23% chose six to eight months, while 12% felt it takes a year or more to heal from a break up. So, as you can see, there are varied opinions, and I could tell many of my respondents had previously felt deep heartache.

> **When asked how long it takes to heal from a break up, respondents said:**
>
> "At least a few weeks, if it was someone I was head over heels about, then a lot longer. It royally sucks if your heart breaks from a break up."
>
> "Two or three weeks." "I usually distract myself until the hurt ends and I fill it with things that I enjoy instead. Dating is meant to have ups and downs. You go through it because you know the end result will be worth it OR you will die trying. Either way, you will feel a little pain on the down turns (but man those mountain peaks are pretty damn amazing)."

Some still felt the sting of heartbreak:

"Sometimes never," said one. "You always think of the person."

"To this day I would love to be with a lover from ten years ago," another replied.

Some people said they wouldn't get over their last relationship until they find a replacement or a distraction. I can see how a distraction may help ease the pain, but if you jump into a rebound relationship quickly after a break up, the chances of it lasting are not very high—unless you're not looking for anything serious.

I saved the best for last (surely, the most entertaining, but not the healthiest).

"The macho thing to say is, it depends on how much cash I have on me and how far away the nearest titty bar is," said one man. "Realistically though, I do heal pretty quickly."

Another agreed.

"About five minutes," he said. "When a relationship ends, I get on with living. Usually I am glad it ended."

Heal your broken heart.

For those of you who are working through the pain: surround yourself with a strong support system. Women are great at this. My girlfriends and I are always there for one another to listen, motivate one another, and give honest feedback when needed. Men are not as in touch with their emotions as women are. Men don't talk to their friends about what they're feeling. Single men are more likely to seek emotional comfort from their mothers, sisters, and female friends.

What can you do to get over your latest love? Sorry, the answer is not to meet someone else the very next day, or while you're still in the relationship and things are starting to go sour (although "meet someone else" was a very popular answer). Here is a list compiled from the information I gathered from the volunteers:

1. Therapy.
2. Fishing.
3. Do anything with friends or family.
4. Learn a new language or how to play an instrument.
5. Bible study group or read my bible.
6. Work out.
7. I focus on my photography, plunge myself into work.
8. Do something creative.
9. Work on myself, join a new club or group or take a trip.
10. Educate myself (read inspirational/motivational books).
11. Drink rum (yes, this was an answer).
12. Focus on the good things of life; see the positive side to the breakup.
13. Improve things about myself.
14. Keep myself busy.
15. Go to social events.
16. Carry on with life.
17. Smile, no matter what is going on when I am out. A smile covers a lot.
18. Head to the spa.
19. Get involved in charities.
20. Mope and sleep for a few days, then go on a diet.

21. Spend time in my yard, do yoga, bike ride, hike with my dogs, write in my journal.
22. My recommendation would be to take care of yourself, nurture your soul, take as much time as needed, and refrain from dating again until you're ready, no matter what other people say.

The key to these suggestions is to get preoccupied with life—get busy. Take action, and refocus your mind. Create enough interests so that the next time you're in a relationship, your life won't be so one-dimensional. The more interests you have, the less you'll rely on your partner to try and fill what may be missing in your life.

Whether you spent six months or twenty-five years with somebody before you went your separate ways, each relationship is still a part of you, as they affect who you are and who you were.

Every experience that adds to our biography helps us to develop in one way or another.

Cherish the good times, grow from the bad times, and remember the quote from Alfred Lord Tennyson, "Tis better to have loved and lost than never to have loved at all."

Chapter Review.

Fred was hot and heavy with his new girlfriend Amy. This was the first woman he had ever been with, who hardly made time to fit him into her busy schedule. If he said one remark which was even the slightest bit condescending, she called him out on it in a heartbeat. She was just the challenge Fred needed.

He actually planned dates, picked her up, and paid without hesitation. When he went out with the guys he still flirted with other women, but he did not take any of their numbers. Fred was happy and his friends didn't recognize him.

Myra's heart was broken. She became very depressed and watched several chic flicks as she looked at pictures of her and Fred. She ordered take out and stayed in her pajamas all weekend. Her workweeks kept her mind off what happened, but her thoughts would still drift throughout the day. She turned down plans with her friends and wondered if she would end up alone forever. Her best friend had heard enough. She showed up at her house after two weekends of excuses and told Myra to get ready because they were going out. Myra tried to resist, but her friend wasn't taking no for an answer. They went out that night and Myra had a good time, but she was still upset. Her friend kept calling and asking her to do fun activities to try to get her out of her despair. Her friend was there to listen over a glass of wine as Myra poured her heart out for hours. After a few more weeks, Myra decided to start doing some things for herself.

She joined the gym and lost a few pounds, got a new haircut and went shopping for some new clothes. She started a journal and got in closer touch with her emotions. As the weeks flew by she started to feel better, took an art class and tried yoga for the first time, which she enjoyed. Myra decided to go to therapy, which she had never done before.

The therapist helped her unearth deep-rooted feelings she had pushed down for a long time, that negatively affected how she felt about herself, and what she deserved. As Myra grew stronger, she looked back at her relationship with Fred, and realized how far she had come.

She came up with a couple of positive affirmations, which she read every night before going to bed. She met a nice man at her art class and they became fast friends. Although he was a great guy, she did not feel he was a good match, and it felt good to be able to make the decision to have a man as a friend that she didn't feel she was compatible with, and yet still enjoyed his company.

Bob and Lanie have been discussing the future and where they would like to live someday. Bob got a promotion at work which they celebrated with their best friends, a couple they have a lot of fun with, relate to, and laugh all night with. Bob started to have pains in his lower abdomen that went on for a few weeks. After he finally told Lanie, she urged him to go the doctors. It hurt when the doctor pushed down on it so he was sent for tests to determine why.

He was diagnosed with appendicitis and needed to have an operation as soon as possible. The operation was scheduled for Friday morning, so Lanie took the day off work to be by his side. The operation went well and when Bob woke up, Lanie was right there. She bought all his favorite foods, ordered a bunch of movies, and took care of him all weekend.

She made his mother's homemade chicken soup recipe which comforted Bob. Although during the long weekend they fought once over the remote, Bob looked at Lanie, and knew at that very moment, she was who he wanted to be by his side permanently.

CHAPTER TEN

We're Just Friends – Really!

It's the age-old question. Can men and women just be friends? Hold your answer, because that's what we're going to dive into now. We're going to investigate every aspect of friendship with the opposite sex: friends with benefits, getting stuck in the "friend zone," other people's thoughts about your friendship, the same friendship with two different viewpoints, and being friends with your ex or not. Personally, I say yes, and some of my closest friends are men, though I sometimes feel men have a harder time with this than women do. I have had close male friendships all my life and cherish them dearly. The only downside is when the other person has different expectations. I've lost wonderful friendships because the other person realized they wouldn't be leaving the "friend zone," so they ended the friendship, which hurt at times. As long as both are on the same page, these friendships can last a lifetime. The funny thing about being a friend with the opposite sex, however, is a lot of the time you have to convince other people in your life that you really are "just friends." I feel it's strange in how it's something you need to convince people about, but there are some people who feel men and women simply cannot be friends. Just like in the movie *When Harry met Sally*, Billy Crystal's character Harry says men and women can't be friends because sex will always get in the way. I have some male friends who are very attractive and people ask me what's wrong with them—as if every man you know should be a potential dating prospect! I have a particular friend my family adores. They were always waiting for me to say I experienced an epiphany in my love life and didn't realize how foolish I had been, because he was right there all along. We've known each other since we were twenty years of age, and years ago he told me his mother wished he would have married me (after he got a divorce). We both laughed because we had not only put one another into the friend zone, we took it a step further and placed one another in the "as close to family as you can get zone," which rules out romance. Last year he re-married and I'm so happy for him. I do understand that in some opposite sex friendships, the male or female friend may be waiting on the sidelines for you to have a weak moment and fall into bed with them one night. A guy I know says men are also hoping that when you break up with someone, they can be that needed shoulder to cry on and in-between the tears they'll be there when you reach out for some "comforting." One of my closest friends admitted to me recently that now she is married, she has lost all her male friends, as if they had fallen off the face of the earth. They simply stopped calling. I have also experienced this in the past when involved in a serious relationship.

Are you sure you're just friends? And so the story goes.

When you're in a relationship, your mate may get uptight about your friends of the opposite sex, and the subject can cause tension if one of the partners is not secure in the relationship. If you've had a friend for many years before seeing this person, your boyfriend or girlfriend should not ask you to give up your friendship with them, just because it makes them uncomfortable. Now, if this is someone you used to sleep with, this could get touchy. You can help them feel more comfortable with the friendship by eventually letting your partner meet that friend so they realize it's simply platonic.

When it came to those I questioned, everyone except for two people felt men and women can be friends! A few people did add that if either the man or woman is physically attracted to the other, the friendship wouldn't work. A couple of the women said that they have more male friends than female friends.

One of the guys feel it is easy for women but not for men, and another pointed out that it's human nature and only a matter of time before a man will try to sleep with his female friend. That doesn't mean they necessarily want to date her, though. Again, men (and even some women) can separate sex and love.

Friends with benefits.

So, you tell me your girlfriend or boyfriend frowns upon your close relationship with your friend of the opposite sex? That the two of you seem a bit too close for comfort and it's hard for them to believe that the friendship is nonsexual, even though they want to trust you?

Although it may be unsettling and you expect your partner to trust you, it may not be improbable to them since "friends with benefits" has become so prevalent.

Unless you have been living under a rock for many years, simply put, a friend with benefits is a person that is just a friend, but both of you also "have sex" together. However, is it really that simple?

For those who watched the movie *Friends with Benefits,* feelings may evolve for both parties. You become a couple, love is professed and violins play, wrapping it up with a pretty bow — this is Hollywood, after all. At other times, one of the players begins to have feelings for the other (often the woman), but the other party is happy to have their cake and to eat it, wanting to remain friends, and the little arrangement will either continue or end. The way I look at it, friends with benefits is like a pit stop until one or both finds the person they really want to be with. I have witnessed some sad situations where someone is into another (they thought they were strong enough just to have them around for a good time, until emotions got in the way), but the feelings were not reciprocated. The one who truly isn't into the other will continue to sleep with them. Hey, they have nothing going on at the moment, right? Sometimes they're being strung along for years, hanging on to the occasional compliment or bit of praise, such as the "I don't know what I would do without you in my life" line, which is a far cry from, "I love you and want to be with you." The wounded bird sits hoping, wishing, praying that one day they're going to tell them everything they ever wanted to hear, and then one harsh morning, they wake up from that dream.

Friends with benefits works for many, especially at a time in one's life when they're not looking for anything serious. As long as both parties are honest and upfront with their expectations and can remain detached, they can be satisfied with this arrangement.

People may tread lightly with friends of the opposite sex they trust, respect, and admire. They're cautious about getting into a relationship with their friend for fear that if it doesn't work out as a couple, they'll lose their valued and possibly closest friend.

I feel friends of the opposite sex are great to have. I personally am in touch with my masculine side, and hanging with the guys can be refreshing. Men are much simpler creatures in the way they view life in general (not saying they are simple), and I appreciate their "no drama" approach. They won't usually break down and talk to their male friends about how distraught they are from their latest break up, but their gal pal will be happy to listen, talk things out, and dissect what went wrong. At times women can get a little too carried away with looking at men and dating in general under a microscope, instead of going with the flow. This is when it's important for women to concentrate on their needs and interests, so they will be too busy to nit-pick their relationship.

In 2012, the researcher April Bleske-Rechek and colleagues from the University of Wisconsin Eau Claire did a study on attraction in cross-sex friendships to see if people viewed these friendships as a benefit or burden. Eighty-eight pairs of undergraduate friends were interviewed and their answers were strictly confidential—going as far as having the friends agree in front of one another that the study would not be discussed after it was completed. The results showed that men were attracted to their female friends a lot more often and overestimated the level of attraction their female friends had for them. In nearly all the cases, they assumed that because they were attracted to their friend, their friend obviously felt the same. Women were generally not attracted to their male friends and underestimated how attracted their male friends were to them. Men were more apt to act on their misperception of their female friends' attraction to them, and the friends' relationship status wasn't relevant. Men desired dates with women who were single and those who were in relationships. Women were sensitive to their male friends' relationship status, and didn't want to pursue their friend if they were involved with someone else.

In the second part of this study, the same researchers interviewed 249 adults and placed them into two separate age categories: one group was made up of ages eighteen to twenty-three, and the second group ranging from twenty-seven to fifty-two years of age, most of whom were married. The researchers questioned the participants about the negative and positive aspects of being friends with a member of the opposite sex. The participants in the first group were more attracted to their friends than the older second group, but this discrepancy disappeared when the participants were single. Single men reported high levels of attraction toward their female friends and single women reported moderate levels of attraction in both age groups. Both agreed that these relationships are more negative than positive because of the possible consequences, especially if attraction was present. Middle-aged men and women that were romantically attracted to their friends reported lower levels of satisfaction in their marriage. Men were more likely to say that romantic attraction to their opposite sex friend was a benefit and this increased with age. Men in the younger group were four times more likely to report a romantic attraction than the younger female participants. The older male participants were ten times more likely than females of the same age to report an attraction. These two studies concluded women more often feel that men and women simply are just platonic friends, but for men, it was more often not the case. Men find it harder to turn off thoughts that someday the friendship may lead to something more.

Both studies make sense and I do feel (being a woman) that a great majority of the time when women place men in the "friend zone," that is all they will ever be, and they're not thinking of their friend as a future possible dating prospect. If a woman is interested in a man, he will know it from the way she behaves around him. Also, there is an unwritten rule among women (not all, but a great amount agree) that their friend's ex-boyfriends, let alone husbands, are not available dating prospects. In a situation where your male friend is in a current relationship, the same rule applies. Even though the woman may not be close or even know her male friend's girlfriend, a high percentage of women wouldn't even think about it—but of course, there are still some who would go for it anyway. Men usually don't feel as bad about going after their female friends (who are in relationships), because their strong level of attraction could sway their moral compasses.

Put yourself in their shoes.

What about this scenario: Would you be jealous if the person you were dating spent time with their very attractive friend of the opposite sex who they have been friends with for years? What about a new friend of the opposite sex they just met and are spending a lot of time with?

More people had a harder time with the latter situation. The first situation with the friend who had been in their life for many years was a 60/40 split, with 60% feeling they wouldn't get jealous, but 40% saying they would. Of course, if you spend a lot of time with your friend verses your mate, inevitably, they would start to feel neglected. As for the other situation with the attractive "new" friend, the results were an 80/20 split.

Eighty percent would have an issue with this new friend manipulating a lot of their partner's life, and 20% felt they would not have a problem.

What about your ex? Can you just be friends?

Personally, there are so many different scenarios attached to this question that there's no easy answer. I feel it's possible and have been friends with a few of my exes, but I have yet to become close friends with men that I have spent multiple years with, though anything is possible. I have known couples who have hung around with their partner's ex-husband or wife and their spouse, proving that some people are meant to come into your life, but sometimes you are definitely better off as friends. They weren't meant to share a life together as a couple, but can remain dear friends. When you are good friends with your ex or exes and you tell your new girlfriend or boyfriend about them, you may get more of a negative reaction than if you told them about your childhood friend of the opposite sex. It takes a very strong relationship for a partner to feel secure when you're spending time with your ex, but it can work if you trust one another completely. Of course, every situation is different, but even the strongest partner may not feel comfortable with you having your ex as a friend. It could be hard for your mate to feel completely secure with their partner "hanging out" with someone they may have loved at one time. As much as they may try or say they are fine with it, even the most trusting partner may have thoughts of the two of you rekindling old feelings you once had, especially with the more time you spend together.

In a situation where someone is still in love and the other has moved on, a friendship would be tough. If the relationship ended badly, friendship probably won't be an option unless you both allow time to pass and have come to a place of true forgiveness. If two people date for a while and realize they are not compatible, I feel they may be able to form a friendship, but if they are largely incompatible, they might not have enough in common to want to pursue it. Seventy percent of the group feels you can be friends with an ex, while 20% felt they could not, and 10% were not sure or felt it depended on the situation. Also, some who felt you can be friends with an ex prefaced the question by stating it is possible in some situations, or with certain people. Women had an easier time becoming friends with their ex, though many stated they couldn't be friends with an ex they once had very strong, deep, loving feelings for.

Chapter Review.

Fred's girlfriend keeps him on his toes. She is involved with a lot of different organizations, works out every day, and sees her friends regularly, which meant he had to ask her out ahead of time, if he wanted to see her. When she didn't give him enough of her time, it made him want her even more. One night, they had plans to go to the movies. Fred waited in front of the theater for forty minutes but she never showed. She didn't call him to let him know why she wasn't there. He texted and called multiple times but all he got was silence and voicemail. Fred went home in a huff. No woman was going to treat him like this.

At midnight, he heard a knock at his door. He opened the door and his girlfriend flashed him a Cheshire cat-like smile. She took off her coat which revealed her tight red dress, shiny black hair cascading down her shoulders. "I got stuck helping someone out after I went out with my friends and lost track of time," she said. He told her how long he waited and how he irritated he was because of how inconsiderate she had been. "I can see how angry you are, Fred, so maybe I should just go."

"You don't have to do that," Fred stated. "I want to spend time with you, but you got me mad."

"Well, I'm here now so why don't you stop talking, and come over here and show me how happy you are to see me," she said. Fred walked over, grabbed and kissed her hard on her mouth, more than happy to oblige.

Myra got set up on a blind date, someone who one of her friends and her husband knew. She didn't feel like going, but pushed herself to go. They met for a few drinks after work; he was not only attractive with a respectable career (fireman) but he was incredibly easy to talk to and very down to earth.

At the end of the date, he walked her to her car and told her what a great time he had, she smiled and said she had a great time as well. Myra called her friend after she pulled away, thanking her for setting her up with such a great guy. The next day, he called to ask her out for Saturday night, and she accepted.

At the restaurant, they got seated at the best table, which was located outside under the stars. The food was sensational and the ambiance was perfect. The sound of classic jazz played in the background. After dinner Bob asked her to take a walk. They held hands and walked down the cobblestone streets that led to a park along the water. The old gas streetlamps lit up the street in shades of yellow and the moon was full and amazing. They walked over to a small waterway bridge and sat on the ledge overlooking the water. Bob got serious and Lanie could tell he was a bit nervous.

He took her hand in his and got down on one bended knee. He took a ring out of his pocket and said, "Lanie, you have made me happier than I thought was possible and I have loved every minute I

> have spent with you. You're my best friend and I want you to be by my side for the rest of our lives. Will you marry me?" Lanie's eyes filled with tears. "Yes," she said with a smile. "I've been waiting for you all my life." They embraced for a long while, then Bob placed the ring on Lanie's finger. They continued their walk and savored every moment of their magical evening.

The heart is a fragile thing. Even if things didn't work out, and you realize it's for the best, a lot of people would have a problem being friends with an ex and hearing about how happy they are with someone else.

Like a dog that marks his territory, even though he found a new favorite spot to place his bone, he still doesn't want the neighbor's dog placing his bone in the old place.

CHAPTER ELEVEN

More Than Once in a Lifetime

"If you found it once you can find it again," I recently declared to a client. Love can be complex and it sometimes arrives when you aren't expecting it. When you are honestly ready it will be easier for it to find and grab hold of you. This chapter is about finding that one special love of your life or perhaps a few great loves over a lifetime. The ability to attract who you want requires looking within and building your tool-box. We will also talk about soul-mates, why people settle, infidelity, and the lessons love has to teach us.

Many people have been fortunate enough to find great love more than once in a lifetime. I've heard stories where someone lost the love of their life who they felt could never be replaced, then eventually someone else entered their life and they had a similar level of love toward them. It is important not to lose hope, because the individual you thought was the love of your life has moved on. Your life isn't over and is filled with opportunity! It's possible to meet one, two, or more people who will make you feel those silly, lovesick feelings, which may eventually lead to a love that will stand the test of time.

The person in the mirror.

Everyone has issues. Define normal, right? No one is perfect and we need to accept that. Take a hard look at yourself and make a list, preferably a written one: What do I love about myself? What are my positive qualities? Where do I excel? What can I bring to a relationship? The list should be easy to compile and if it isn't, here's a freebie—you need to work on your self-esteem. Unknowingly, we attract problems, situations, and incompatible partners into our life because of one immense problem: **People don't love themselves enough**. Now, let's look at the negatives. If you could change five things about yourself, what would they be? What areas of your life need improvement? Where are your weaknesses in your relationships?

Remember, it's all about baby steps. Rapid change isn't going to happen overnight. A quote I came up with for my business, "Even a small step toward change is a step in the right direction." As hard as it is to change, this is the only way to grow and expand your thought processes. You can learn to empower yourself and remove those weights that have been bearing down on you. However, you must be willing to do the work.

Your personal toolbox.

Where do I start? I want to change, but where do I begin? Everyone's likes and dislikes vary, so you must customize your path to meet your needs. You are your greatest asset, but to become a better partner you must first get in touch with yourself. Become comfortable in your own skin and don't worry about what others say. Some individuals put on a false persona because they are afraid of being judged. If you can be real in all facets of your life, your life will be more content because there are a lot of people who struggle to be genuine. If you can get to a place where you're living your "authentic" life, full of self-love and joy, and can be happy, whether you are alone or with someone, you will have mastered the ultimate challenge and given yourself the greatest gift. Healthy self-appreciation is the epitome of self-mastery.

There are so many different mediums that will produce change. I'm going to share some of those areas so you can pick and choose what works best. We are going to start with **personal affirmations**, as well as **self-hypnosis**. Did you ever hear the saying, "If you hear it enough, eventually you start to believe it?" Sadly, people making this statement are usually referring to negative statements about themselves they heard from someone or more than one person, multiple times. Eventually, those hurtful words become ingrained in their mind, which in turn affects their self-image. You can re-program your thoughts with positive affirmations. Your subconscious mind doesn't have the ability to differentiate between thoughts that are real and those that are not, thoughts we believe and those we don't. Everything we take in is registered, so choose your thoughts wisely. The late Dr. Susan Jeffers (psychologist and author) and the recently departed, Louise Hay (motivational author and founder of Hay House) teach us just how powerful affirmations are. Think about something you currently don't believe about yourself that you want to implement into your life and write it down in a journal, an index card, or a piece of paper. Make sure you frame it in a positive tense. A few examples might be: "I am worthy and capable of giving and receiving love," "My heart is filled with peace and joy," or "I am smart and successful." You can tailor your affirmations to whatever you want to work on. Before you go to bed each night and are starting to unwind, turn off the noise in your head and read each affirmation at least three times. Your unconscious mind is most open to receive input at this time. There are many books loaded with great personal affirmations if you're having a hard time coming up with your own. Like affirmations, self-hypnosis is simply shutting off your thoughts for a bit while you relax and take in positive information. You download the MP3s to your computer or IPod, can buy CDs, or there are self-hypnosis apps for your phone. You close your eyes and listen to a voice in the background that will help guide you toward changing whatever you choose.

Journaling.

Pouring out your deepest thoughts on paper is very healing, with your feelings meeting the crisp page. You may also want to write down positive quotes, poems and so on. Letter writing is another wonderful tool that releases negative emotions to those from your past that have hurt you, or you have hurt. It helps to write to release pain you have not worked through. Write a letter to the person who hurt you, expressing all the pain you suffered, or the guilt you're letting go of from the hurt you may have caused somebody else. You don't need to mail the letters; this is about processing the feelings on your own. After you have done so, if you feel you really need to send the letter and are ready to do so, send it as a token of closure without any expectations. You don't want to set yourself up to experience more pain by expecting an apology you may never get.

Music.
Songs emote feelings from the words that resonate with us. Listen to music that touches something deep inside you, something you may have not been in touch with in quite some time.

Books.
There is a book out there for any problem or issue you need to work through. You name the emotion, you'll find it.

Emotional Freedom Technique or "Tapping."
This technique is based on the principal that we and everything surrounding us is made up of energy. We each have meridians (energy pathways) in our bodies, and when these vessels get disrupted or blocked by negative emotions, that energy gets stuck or trapped. Tapping (EFT) is a way of releasing this negative energy. It uses only twelve of these pathways, making the sequence you go through when practicing easy to master. You tap on these meridians, with two fingers, as you state positive messages about yourself and what you want to address. Trapped negative energy can cause mental or physical issues. When your body is not at ease you are more susceptible to disease entering your body. Hence, your body is in a state of dis-ease. You can find out more about EFT/tapping online, or in books and other materials on the subject. Gary Craig is the founder of EFT. Check out his website at: http://www.emofree.com. Brad Yates and Nick Ortner are also two EFT experts you may want to follow, if you're interested in learning more.

Meditation.
If you want to get to a deeper level of oneness and calm, meditation is the call. Sit with your legs crossed or together and in front of you, with your

palms either up or down on your lap. Clear your mind and concentrate on deep, diaphragmatic breathing. It's hard for some people to focus, so practice makes perfect. You can concentrate on a mantra if that's easier for you, it's very beneficial. If you still feel you're unable to do so, you can purchase meditation downloads, CDs and so on where you can follow along with someone in a guided mediation. There are also groups you can join. I belonged to one for a couple of years about eight years ago, and when I walked out the door, my body was so relaxed I felt like a noodle.

Therapy and support groups.
Working one on one with an objective party who is trained in the area you are struggling with is beneficial. A therapist can help you explore things you have not been able to see or realize about yourself or your relationships. They will be there to lend an empathetic ear, and will simply listen without judgment. Support groups are helpful because you're able to feel the comradery with others that have or are currently experiencing similar issues. There is something to be said for feeling part of a larger whole.

There are so many ways to produce change and/or heal. I have given you many suggestions to help get you started on your path toward transformation. If you feel you have some concerns that need to be addressed or you simply need to relax more.

Two of my favorite spiritual leaders are Deepak Chopra and the late Dr. Wayne Dyer. Both have an abundance of materials that are well worth checking out.

Chose whatever tools feel comfortable for you (if any) and remember change is hard but doable. Like I tell my clients, some of the communication patterns or behaviors you have been engaging in have most likely been repeated for many years, so to start communicating and behaving differently will feel very strange at first. Give yourself credit and reward yourself for your progress every step of the way. Rewards are not only for children. For instance, for every support group you have pushed yourself to attend, do something you enjoy afterwards to motivate yourself. Be proud of yourself and your growth. When you start feeling better you will shine. When you step out, head held high, radiating self-confidence, people will be drawn to you. Self-confidence is very sexy.

Lastly, believing in a higher power, whether it is God, Buddha, or the new found strength that resides inside you, can help get you through even the darkest times. Appreciate and be thankful for what you have every day.

So many single people complain that they want to meet the right man or women and it seems that they're a magnet for partners that are not suitable for them. The law of attraction states, "like attracts like" and what you haven't dealt with inside is what you're putting out into the universe. Think of it as karma. The partners you pick are a reflection of you.

Those who are lucky in love are not successful because they're lucky, it's because they're in a good place mind, body, and soul. They have their act together, are comfortable in their own skin, love themselves on the inside and outside, and genuinely like people. It shows by their actions, and when they have a problem, they communicate. They usually have a mature attitude, and, even if it's tough, face problems head on and try to stick to the motto, "treat others the way you would like to be treated."

Who wouldn't want to date someone like that? Well, you would be surprised. Like does attract like, so someone who is consistently down on their luck would probably want to delete Suzie Sunshine or Happy Harry out of their phone right after a first date because they're not able to relate to them. They saying *misery loves company* applies here.

Some people are out to change the world one relationship at a time. They're not happy with their partner the way they are, so they make it their mission to turn them into the partner they want them to be. Why fix yourself when trying to fix someone else is so much more fun? So they think. We all know you can't fix someone else. But with some people, the crazier and unhealthier the partner, the better, which makes them feel more comfortable. They recognize likeness, their fractured equal, as if there was something pulling these two individuals toward one another. In most cases, there actually is, and it's the unconscious need to keep reliving an unfinished relationship from their past. A woman may have never felt love from her father and no matter what she did to please him, it was never good enough. She may seek out partners who say they don't want to be in a relationship and don't think she's special to only try to change their view. She will win their heart and admiration, therefore succeeding at getting love from a man, which she was unable to receive from her father. The more challenging the better. In most cases, so much of what we do is unconscious, and she's most likely not even aware she's doing this.

Loneliness plays a part as well, as we looked at earlier. I have witnessed people hang onto a crazy relationship just to avoid being alone. People want someone by their side; they can't handle being alone.

Can you be completely alone, or do you always tend to be in a relationship?

Ninety three percent of those I questioned said they can be alone and don't always need to be with someone, but many people admitted it's hard at times. The length of time that people spend alone isn't so considerable. I loved what Virginia had to say: "I like myself! I find it very easy to be alone as I enjoy my own company."

I feel if more people liked themselves and enjoyed being alone, they wouldn't be in unhealthy relationships.

Mario said, "I can. I'm comfortable being alone, but I have no doubt that a man was born to have a woman by his side." Very chivalrous!

Getting back to the thought of true, everlasting love, I know people who got it right the first time. There are couples who were meant to be. They found their one true love and this person just fits. They feel more at home with this person than any other, and would go to the ends of the earth for them. Being without their beloved would leave too much emptiness. Parting would bring deep sorrow, and heartbreaking stories are told. You get couples who have been together for many years and deeply loved one another, but then one partner dies. Shortly thereafter, their partner/spouse dies of a broken heart. This person could have been the object of health and they end up dying because life to them no longer seemed worth living. The legendary Johnny Cash is a great example, passing away only four months after he lost his beloved June Carter-Cash. She was his main reason for living. One of his famous quotes was, "This morning with her, having coffee." His description of paradise.

In 2011 the University of Saint Andrews published a longitudinal study that followed 58,000 couples from the early '90s. The findings proved that within the first six months after a spouse's death, their spouse had a 40% higher risk of death and for a decade following the death the risk of death also increases. Forty percent of men and 26% of women died within three years after their partners' passing.

Some couples surprise us; there are couples who seem to argue a lot, but are still powerfully united and when trouble comes, they stand strong. Those who say they never disagree are the ones you need to question. There aren't a lot of people who agree on everything. It's just not realistic. I'm not saying lots of arguing is healthy, don't get me wrong—you just need to be able to share and discuss your differences and feelings.

Corny as this may sound, some couples really do complement one another. There are harmonious couples that make love seem effortless.

I believe in soul mates, and believe in loving different people in different ways. You can have more than one great love and can have one that makes you feel like no other. Being in tune with someone on a whole other level and being privileged to share their innermost thoughts and dreams is the ultimate feeling. It's a great feeling when you feel safe enough with someone to be open, raw and exposed, and to know they're there for you no matter what, always wanting the best for you. American writer Richard Bach said, "A soul-mate is someone who has locks that fit our keys, and keys to fit our locks. When we feel safe enough to open the locks, our truest selves step out and we can be completely and honestly who we are; we can be loved for who we are and not for who we're pretending to be. Each unveils the best part of the other. No matter what else goes wrong around us, with that one person we're safe in our own paradise."

Let's go to the polls on soul mates. To believe, or not to believe? Sixty eight percent of the people I asked do believe, 36% do not, and 5% were unsure. What do you believe?

I recently read a great story about a 72-year-old woman who got married for the first time because she finally felt she'd met her soul mate! Now, that's a woman who truly wouldn't settle. You're never too old to fall in love; adopt patience, assert faith, and imagine!

I'm a firm believer that some people do want the "real deal"— a love they alone would recognize as no other, but as the years go by and it doesn't happen, they end up settling for the next best offer. Everyone around them may be getting married, and it seems like the next logical step in their relationship, so they figure it's better to be with someone than to take the chance of being alone for the rest of their life. So, reluctantly, they get married. They may feel their partner is a great person, a good cook, has enough money to support them, a comfortable roommate, and many other things. But there is a price for settling. There's always a tradeoff. They still must lie next to their partner every night. At times women want the wedding so badly, they look at their partner with one eye shut, because they want their lifelong goal to become a reality. I've known people who stay until something better comes along because they have someone keeping them warm at night, and feel that even inadequate attention is better than no attention. It can also be they simply can't stomach the thought of being alone. Women may settle because they want children and their biological clock is ticking loudly. Here's a switch: at a cook-out I attended recently, a 35-year old male colleague was having a conversation with two other women and myself, and admitted to feeling his clock ticking. He said although he didn't have to worry about his biological clock in the same way as a woman, he was adding up how much time it may take to find someone he wants to marry, how long they would need to date before they got married and how long they may wait before they had children. He finally said he wants to be young enough to run around with his kids and he felt like he was running out of time. So even though the pressure is not placed on men as much as women, they still think about it on some level. I've known many women and men with mothers who drive them crazy about settling down, getting married, and having kids. However, if you settle, you may be signing up for years of mediocre happiness or possible misery. This is not the way to live, but people usually prefer to be in with the norm and not the exception. Living in a lonely marriage is far worse than simply being alone.

What happens years later when the right one does come along and it's too late, because you chose to settle? It depends on the person's moral compass. Some have done right by their partner and stayed. (I am a movie buff and the movie *Bridges of Madison County* comes to mind. By the way, it's Marlon Wayans favorite movie which I heard on *The Queen Latifah Show*.) With divorce as simple as it is today, many will leave to be with the one they love or think they love. Eight-eight percent of those asked feel people do settle in their relationships and had some pretty strong opinions about the subject.

> ### Do people settle in relationships? Here's what the volunteers had to say:
>
> "Yes, this happens all the time and is a HUGE mistake. If people were more comfortable with themselves, this would not happen."
>
> "I believe people are sick of being single, but more likely afraid of growing old alone. Rarely do I see examples of healthy relationships, which makes me wonder if it is a realistic goal."
>
> There were a lot of remarks about people being lonely and "not loving themselves enough," as I have noted over and over throughout this book.
>
> "I feel a lot of the time people marry due to societal pressures."
>
> Two of the men feel this is why the divorce rate is so high. One of the ladies agreed and said it drives her crazy.
>
> One female volunteer stated that scared and insecure people settle.
>
> Some other thoughts were:
>
> "I think people don't want to wait and see what is out there, or they think what they have is as good as it will get."
>
> "I feel I should just say yes to someone who accompanies me and likes me even though I have no intention of ever being in love with them.

> You have to assess the situation and realize that love has to come first before a big step."
>
> "Yes, indeed I feel most people get married because it's convenient for them. That's the only one reason I think can explain a lot of people getting married in their early 20s."
>
> "We have been desensitized to real life, and prefer to live the life society tells us is "good," which includes being straight, married, wealthy, a purebred, being a couple of the same race, etcetera.

Responding to the last comment, you would think society would have evolved so considerably that we wouldn't have to be concerned with people's opinions on such matters today, but it still happens. We have to try to ignore unsolicited opinions and live our lives the way we want, as long as we are not hurting anyone (especially ourselves).

In 2013 at the Siemens Festival Nights in London (a unique three-day event showcasing three different operas with incredible special effects) 2,000 people were surveyed about their romantic and sexual histories. The results showed that one in seven people or as many as 73% <u>didn't</u> think the person they're currently dating or are married to was the love of their life. They claimed to be "making do" with their partner because their true love got away. This definitely supports what I've thought all along about the hoppers! Forty-six percent said they would be prepared to leave their current partner to be with their true love (hopper in action). The men in the study were more loyal to their partners, with 37% saying they would stay in the relationship for their partner's sake. Credible, and to me, it makes sense. It has been statistically proven that men stay in relationships longer than women when they're unhappy. Men can become complacent and usually don't need as much to make them happy (again embracing life in drama free fashion), so some choose to settle for a mediocre level of happiness. As discussed in chapter nine, a man often puts off breaking up with a woman longer than the opposite, for fear of hurting her or her possible adverse reaction. If a man is having sex on a regular basis, he may overlook other issues. Men lose out on having the comfort of someone nurturing them when single, whereas women have strong support systems through their friends and female family members. Even if the couple doesn't get along most of the time, remember what I said earlier about the comfort that comes with the devil you know being better than the one you don't. Let's face it, dating requires a lot of effort. Also, when a man thinks about losing his security, family, and the financial burden he may incur when leaving (if he's married), he may feel it's a logical decision to stay. Women will often leave when they're not getting their emotional needs met, but there are also women that will stay for the wrong reasons. Some are willing to leave and see where the cards may fall, all for the possibility of an amazing future love. The Siemen's study results are discouraging, but not shocking. Seventeen percent said they met their true love since they got together with their current mate. A whopping 60% said it took just ten weeks to know if someone was the one. Like I said, "You won't have to question it, you'll just know." The average person in the 2013 study fell in love twice in their lifetime, but those polled at the festival in 2012 (2,000 adults as well) fell in love on an average of four times.

This study also revealed that women fall in love more often than men (probably not a major shocker to most), and although true love is hard to find, the majority claimed that even though they were not with their true love they said they were head over heels with their current partner. Well, at least people do feel they're in a better than average relationship, but just imagine for a moment that most of those people decided not to just "make do," and more people decided instead to wait for the love of their life to come along. People waste years in mediocrity when they could have been with a love they were more compatible with. I understand these relationships provide companionship, good times and fill up lonely moments, but people know sooner rather than later when they're with someone who they don't have strong feelings for. Can you imagine the level of happiness people would feel and the positive impact it would make! The world would be filled with more of the positivity it's starving for.

Dr. Carmen Harra, Ph.D. (intuitive psychologist, author, relationship coach), wrote a great article about soul mates. Dr. Harra agrees that too many people settle. She claims she sees a lot of people who settled down due to financial reasons, children, family influence and social status, and some didn't want to go through the pain of breaking up, only to start from scratch again. She also claimed, as I have, that she feels people don't ultimately want to end up alone.

In her article "Soul Mate or Life Partner? Ten Elements of a Soul Mate" Dr. Harra named ten signs that the love you're experiencing is a soulmate connection.

> *It's something inside*: it's a tenacious, profound and lingering emotion, which no words can encompass.

> *Flashbacks*: you might feel an odd sense of déjà vu, as if the moment in time has already taken place, perhaps a long time ago, and perhaps in a different setting.

> *You just get each other*: Ever met two people who finish each other's sentences? It is a telltale sign of a soulmate when you experience it with your partner.

> *You fall in love with his (or her) flaws*: soulmates have an easier time of accepting and even learning to love each other's imperfections.

> *It's intense*: even during negative episodes, you're focused on resolving the problem, and can see beyond the bad moment.

> *You two against the world*: soulmate relationships are founded on compromise and unity above all else.

> *You're mentally inseparable*: soulmates have a mental connection similar to twins.

> *You feel secure and protected*: your soulmate will make you feel like you have a guardian angel by your side.

You can't imagine your life without him (or her): a soulmate is not someone you can walk away from that easily.

You look each other in the eye: looking a person in the eye when speaking denotes a high level of comfort and confidence.

I must say, as much as I believe in soulmates, you also need to focus on remaining grounded in your ideals. A lot of literature warns people that although the term "soulmate" seems lovely, it can also cause people to have issues finding a mate or functioning in the day-to-day workings of a relationship. Being an effective couple is like a full-time job and both need to work at it daily. Problems can arise when people have false representations of how couples are supposed to be, such as watching romantic movies that portray people happy in love, showing they have a cosmic connection which can get them through even the worst of times with little effort. Many also think the way they felt in the honeymoon period will last forever and everything will be perfect. Perfection doesn't exist, and, like Dr. Harra pointed out, soulmates learn to embrace their love even with their imperfections. Your partner's unique traits and quirks (even the annoying ones) make them who they are.

Some of the saddest stories I have heard involve someone who has been in a relationship for many years, then the relationship begins to stagnate or the couple goes through an incredibly rough patch. Someone eventually gets a lot of attention from an outside party, ends up being unfaithful, and feels for a short time that the grass is greener on the other side. They get stars in their eyes, think about that person throughout the day, anticipating the next meeting with their new love, and indeed feel they have found their soulmate. You know where I'm going with this one, right? They leave their current relationship and dive in head first into their new relationship until the newness wears off, and problems (very possibly the same problems they had in their previous relationship) start to surface. After a while, things fizzle out and they realize how much they miss their previous partner and can't stop thinking about them. They conclude that they were with their soulmate all along, but just didn't see it at the time because they were knee-deep in problems, and blinded by the wrong assumption that life should be problem-free when it comes to human interactions. They end the relationship and try to win back the love of their life, and some are given a second chance, but others aren't so lucky. Cheating is the ultimate betrayal of trust in a relationship. Many relationships have been destroyed because of a hot night of passion or an affair that may have gone on for years, before the guilty culprit was caught. It takes a strong individual to forgive such a deed, but in certain circumstances, the relationship can end up stronger, if the couple works hard at mending what needed fixing in the first place. I have worked with people who eventually, were able to say their relationship was stronger than ever, after surviving an affair.

Recently, a friend told me a story about a guy she was seeing years ago. He just happened to be the only guy her family has liked thus far; he was a smooth talker and everyone bought his act. He was a dentist with two practices, and had three children. He had been going through a divorce for years, which was a red flag my friend missed. If someone you date is not already divorced for at least a year (because you want to make sure they had enough time to process through their feelings regarding the divorce), it's wise to tell them to call you in the future and wish them well.

This guy wined and dined my friend, took her to fabulous restaurants and amazing trips, and they could talk about anything all night until the sun came up. Unfortunately, in a year of their time together, she never met his children, which she thought was odd. She didn't see him every weekend because he had them every other weekend. There was always a reason why she hadn't met them and his sweet-talking ways continued to buy him more time. He also was very busy with work and talked about opening another practice. My friend felt a little nudge, letting her know something just wasn't quite right, but she hoped she was wrong. One night, she was at work and she got a call from a woman asking her if she knew who she was. My friend replied she didn't, and the woman proceeded to tell her that she was his girlfriend! They had been dating for two years and she had met his children many times, and explained why my friend had not. They compared stories and both could put together all the pieces to the puzzle. The other girlfriend was never told anything about the possible third practice and all the time spent on making it possible. To this day, my friend thinks the third practice was a third woman, or fourth if you want to count the wife he still wasn't divorced from. The gaps of time when he wasn't with either of them and was supposedly working on this imaginary business made sense. It reminds me of the movie, *The Other Woman,* which was hilarious. It's about a married man who was having an affair with three different women. The wife got wise, befriended the two of them, devised a plan and confronted him, which made for a very entertaining ending.

I have to say, what really got me shaking my head in disbelief from my friend's story was not her smooth-talking boyfriend and everything he got away with, but the fact she told me his parents had met both women, and when they went on vacation, they bought them both separate presents from their trip! Can you say the apple didn't fall far from that tree?

I'm not a fan of reality TV shows, but there are a couple I watch occasionally. *Millionaire Matchmaker* is one — that's very entertaining, to say the least. Last week, Patti had a guy on the show who was a playboy with major commitment issues. She brought on two older gentlemen to open his eyes to his current lifestyle choices. One of the guys was in his mid-seventies and married when he was in his twenties, but ended up cheating and got a divorce. He never married again because he couldn't find anyone who measured up to his ex-wife, and lived with regret for decades. The second man married in his early 40s for the first time and is still very happily married. There is a lot to think about when it comes to finding your ultimate mate. You may want to settle and then regret it when the right one comes along, but we also need to recognize the right one when they're standing in front of us. We need to be careful when boxing people into our idealization of our perfect mate, because our standards might be too high for anyone to meet.

What does your first love say about you?

Remember your first love? Everyone had a different experience, but remembering how you felt when you fell in love for the first time can be bittersweet. Remember that calm, relaxed feeling when you were together, thinking you could conquer the world and nothing else mattered? You probably allowed that person to know you like no one has ever known you before. That relationship was your very first taste of how enchanting love can be. The outcome of that relationship also impacts you in many ways. Maybe you're married to your first love and you have grown together over time. Maybe they were the one that got away due to immaturity or circumstance at the time, and you still think about them to this day. Or maybe the relationship just didn't work out, but you learned some valuable lessons along the way.

According to Dr. Malcolm Brynin, principal research officer at the Institute for Social and Economic Research at the University of Essex, first love paves the way for future relationships. In *Changing Relationships*, a collection of sociological reviews published in 2012, Brynin argued that first relationships become so idealized, they set up unrealistic benchmarks for subsequent relationships. He said that ideally, you would benefit if you could skip your first relationship and wake up in your second relationship, quoting Jane Austen (she is one of my favorites): "Preserve yourself from a first love and you need not fear a second."

Your first experience grabs hold of you and prepares you to love again. If the relationship ended badly, you may enter your next relationship with ambivalence. Experiences build on one another, so one positive experience followed by another positive experience (in this case the relationship) will start to solidify, so that even if two people aren't meant to be and the relationship didn't work out, love is still a wonderful thing. If the first relationship ended badly (and especially if this relationship was turbulent throughout), and the next relationship is followed by another negative experience, you may feel that people cannot be trusted, love is painful, and in turn a shield is placed in front of your tender heart.

Chapter Review.

Fred has been in a relationship that has lasted longer than a year for the first time. He has been calling his girlfriend lately, but she hasn't been returning his calls. He doesn't see her often either because she is always busy, which they argue about. He tried calling today, but the call went straight to voicemail. A few hours later, he tried again and she still didn't respond. The next day when she called, Fred asked her when they would be able to get together. She said she had a lot going on and didn't know when, but she would call when her schedule turned around. Fred went out with the guys after work. He told them what his girlfriend said and they informed him that she is clearly blowing him off. Fred drank a lot and obviously wasn't happy. He drunk dialed her many times but she didn't pick up. He left her messages that appeared more desperate as the night went on. The next morning Fred felt horrible; his head was pounding from last night's shots and he still hadn't heard from her. He texted then called, but only quiet filled the room. Work that day was rough but he made it through the day. The call finally came that evening. His girlfriend stated it wasn't going to work out between them. No real explanation, she felt they weren't right for one another. The next week, Fred's friend saw her holding hands with someone else at a local watering hole. Fred had been seen at his favorite bar drowning his sorrows a few days later, turning on his charm to someone new.

Myra is now in a relationship with someone that treats her very well. Her blind date turned out to be her best date yet and she has been with her boyfriend for over a year. After they had been together a few months, he took her to an exhibit at the Natural History Museum, and told her he loved her while they were looking at the North American Mammal Exhibit. Myra said it back and they hugged in front of the big brown bears. They spend a lot of time together and get along well. They went on a cruise together for a week and had a great time unwinding, dancing, and shopping on the islands. Whenever Myra feels the need to do too much, she imagines a stop sign and relaxes instead. She is determined to get this relationship right, one day at a time. She has let her partner pursue her and lead the way, but remains independent and takes the lead occasionally as well by planning special dates. She is extremely happy, hopelessly in love, and looking forward to an amazing future.

> Bob and Lanie choose to have an intimate evening outdoor wedding at a small winery at the beginning of June. They took a year to plan every detail. Twinkle lights were strung through the trees and gorgeous flowers in mason jars and rose pedals lined the isle. Only their closest friends and family were invited and many stayed at a nearby hotel.
>
> Those attending would be able to take a personalized wine tour the next day. Lanie looked beautiful in a long silk strapless gown. Bob waited anxiously next to the pastor. When he saw Lanie he gasped in awe. Her father walked her down the aisle, and she beamed with happiness as the overwhelming feeling of love she had for Bob swept over her. As they exchanged their vows they both got a bit emotional and felt more connected than ever before. They celebrated with everyone they loved until late in the evening. They went to Paris for their honeymoon and had the time of their lives. It was the first time Bob had ever been to Europe. They embraced the romance the city evoked as they explored the magnificent sights. A year later they took out the two pieces of wedding cake they had frozen from their wedding. They popped open a bottle of bubbly and toasted their one-year anniversary. "Here's to many great years to come," Bob said. "Definitely, you're stuck with me" Lanie said with a smile, as she kissed him repeatedly.

Love has a way of drawing you in and as scary as it may be to some, love can conquer all if you trust it. Even under direst circumstances, you can find your way back to love. You can change your future to reflect more positive relationships, and in time, the love of a lifetime. You may have had many pleasing involvements and wonder why none of them went the distance. Many of the people we date will not end up being our long-term partners, but they teach us many lessons along the way. They can open up our hearts and our minds to many new experiences.

I have been in love a few times and these relationships taught me so much. They filled my life with rich, wonderful experiences that I will always hold close to my heart. I grew exponentially through them. Although ultimately, they weren't the right situations for me, I still believe that the right person is out there and he will enter my life when the time is right. And in the meantime, I enjoy every day and celebrate my single self.

Remember to be open to the possibility of an incredible love entering your life, with an attitude of positive expectations. In other words, be an open receptacle—welcome love in! Use what you have learned in past relationships to see both good and bad signs, so you recognize what worked and what didn't.

If you have been in love once, twice or even multiple times, but still haven't found the absolute love of your life, take a deep breath and hold on to your faith, because you never know what or who is waiting for you around the corner.

CHAPTER TWELVE

The Crazy Things We Do for Love

❦

"One word frees us of all the weight and pain of life. That word is love."
—Sophocles, Greek playwright,
c. 496–406 BC.

In this final chapter, I will be discussing LOVE. I'll talk about what defines it, people's thoughts surrounding it, what makes it last over time and what people have done in the name of love.

Love: people literally go from one end of the earth to the other in search of it. Some have lost their lives over it, and still others are unsure if it even exists. Love can make you feel like you're floating on a cloud, will get you excited to see one another after time apart, and can make people do all sorts of crazy things.

Once established, a loving relationship needs to be worked on daily, cultivated and attended to, but when you're in a wonderful partnership the benefits are definitely worth it.

I'm a very passionate person about so many different aspects of my life, but love to me exemplifies the word "passion."

There are people who chose not to put any effort into their relationships. They think they're supposed to coast on cruise control, and then there are others that will do whatever it takes to make their partner happy. Life is hectic, so hectic that the average married couple is only having sex once a week (up until a couple of years ago it was twice). According to research published in the Newsweek magazine, "Married couples say they have sex an average of 68.5 times a year. That's slightly more than once a week." Regardless of whether you are having sex once a week or five times a day, your relationship needs to be at the top of your list.

A few of my favorite movies include *The Notebook*, *The Vow*, and the classic, *An Affair to Remember,* which was so fabulous that three different versions of the movie were made, demonstrating just how strong the bond between two people can be.

I remember when I was in graduate school, the professor asked the class what we thought were the two components that couples needed to stand the test of time. We all threw out different guesses, each person sure the two answers they chose had to be the right ones. Well, to torture us a little longer, my professor stated at the end of class that he would tell us the answer the next day!

So, the next day after letting us grovel, we finally got the answer. The couples that made it through thick and thin, who celebrate those silver and gold wedding anniversaries, were <u>able to communicate well</u> and were <u>able to resolve conflict before it got out of hand</u>. So, there you have it. Dr. John Gottman discovered this after spending many years working with thousands of couples. Dr. Gottman has a 90% success rate when guessing which couples will go the distance and which will divorce, joking that he and his wife don't get invited out to dinner very often. Many of us in class (including myself) guessed communication, but no one guessed conflict resolution. After I thought about it, I realized how much sense it made. To be able to respect and embrace your differing opinions, work through problems, compromise, and walk away if needed, before things ever escalated. When working with couples I make it a point to talk about how utterly important having respect for your partner is for the health and longevity of the relationship. As soon as the respect starts to fade, the flood gates are open and you'll start to drown. The relationship slowly starts slipping away and needs to be rescued. Your strength will weather storms. Walls aren't usually created when both of you hold one another in the highest regard, even on a day when you're not particularly thrilled with the way your partner is acting.

I asked my trusted volunteers what they thought were the two most important components in making a relationship work.

They came up with many different combinations.

Here are the top five picks:

1. Trust and communication.
2. Trust and honesty.
3. Trust and respect.
4. Communication and respect.
5. Love and respect.

Seventy-five percent of all combinations included one of the above words, trust being a top choice for obvious reasons.

Just like a favorite recipe that contains many delicious ingredients to bring you that mouthwatering bite, love that goes the distance embodies many different elements which over time may need to be fine-tuned, curtailed or expanded, based on awareness of the issues that arise.

Hollywood has cranked out oodles of memorable love stories. Advertisers feed off the concept, and there are multiple songs written about both the joy and heartbreak of love.

When you do a Google search and type in this four-letter word, over 500 million results pop up! Love is everywhere.

There are many different forms of love. We all have the capacity to love many people in our lives, and then there's the kind of love that overwhelms the heart, making it flutter.

Personally, love has always been easy to define. You either love the person or you don't, and there are many different types and levels associated with it. Some people have a very hard time trying to figure out if they are in love, if they've ever truly loved another, and what love specifically means to them. To help clear up the confusion, one may want to make a detailed list of what they see or recognize as "love." In some cases, people are so detached and guarded from their feelings, confusion sets in. Fear also plays a big part. Many people worry about falling in love, and if they do, they fear not having their feelings reciprocated. What if it doesn't work out and I get hurt? Life is full of possibilities, but a life worth living is also full of risks. A life frozen by fear is not worth living in my book, but to so many, there is something to be said for playing it safe. Great love involves great risk, but you must be brave enough to gamble with your fragile heart.

So, have you ever been in love? That crazy, I-would-do-anything-for-the-person, you-can-feel-it-right-down-to- your-toes kind of love? You think about them every day and still get excited when they call, even after you've been together for a long time?

I hope you have and I hope if you are fortunate enough to have found it, you hang onto it tightly.

Almost everyone questioned in my group said they had been in love, and some have been multiple times.

Only four people questioned had never been in love. Three said, "I think so," one stated, "Hard to say," and last but not least, Gabriel said, "Anything is possible."

Here are some of my favorites:

Paul said he had been in love, but couldn't put his finger on what that meant. "To define love—who knows!"

David stated, "It is the most amazing life experience there is. To love someone else so deeply and have that feeling reciprocated is truly amazing."

Todd wrote, "I have been in love before but I don't think that I realized it." Again, proving love can be very confusing.

Rachel said she was currently in love with someone she was dating. "Telling a person you're dating that you love them is a big step. I'm not one to take that lightly."

My favorite quote was from Emiliya (22), who referenced a lyric from a song by the band Sublime, "If you only knew all the love that I found, it's hard to keep my soul on the ground." She went on to say, "Yes, I fall in love often. I love life, and I'm so thankful and happy."

How important is the ring?

As we discussed earlier, fewer people are getting married now than at any time in history.

Some people think of marriage as a goal after they've been with their partner for a reasonable amount of time, with women being the bigger cheerleader for the importance of marriage.

I once was told by a man I was friends with that if a man could have sex every day and never marry the woman, that would be his choice.

Do you think a couple who has been together for many years should get married, or keep things the same, like the quote coined by Burt Lance, "If it ain't broke, don't fix it?" (I always supplement the "ain't" with "isn't" but that was the original phrase.)

There were many different opinions, but the majority of people (including myself) feel it is completely up to the two people involved, whatever works for them. I do have to say, though, I am a strong supporter of marriage if it is right, but at the end of the day, a piece of paper does not define any relationship.

When asked if people should get married after dating a long while, the volunteers replied:

"Get Married. Marriage is not an attempt to fix something that's broken, it's an expression of the life you've developed together and your love for each other. If marriage ruins your serious relationship, then I would guess it was already broken."

"Marriage is just a legal formality. It's not that I don't believe in it, but you don't really need it to prove the two of you really are a couple."

"If the relationship is strong and solid leave it alone."

> "Only those two people can answer the need, or better yet the desire, to legalize their union by all means, so it should come from desire, not need. Need is just satisfying someone else's desire."
>
> "They should allow the relationship to evolve naturally, not change things because of some arbitrary time line."
>
> "I am a huge fan of not letting a piece of paper mess things up. Paper means nothing in this day and age, and I would hate to go through $5,000 of wedding expenses. I would rather just live together, be happy, and if something down the road changes, even in five years, people change, then either reconfigure the relationship or move on."
>
> I loved this one — short, sweet, and to the point:
> "Today's world — go for what makes things work!"

It's true. Today, relationships come in so many different colors, shapes, and sizes. There are so many different types of relationships as well as families! You shouldn't feel you have to conform to someone else's idea of what relationship is right for you. Only you know in your heart what and who is ultimately correct for you. You may disappoint your friend, mother or cousin, but it's your life and you can't please everyone all the time.

Be concerned though if everyone close to you doesn't care for or trust the person you're with. They may see something you don't, or that either consciously or unconsciously you're unaware of. It may be something you haven't worked through that is drawing you to this person, or something about them that you can't see but really need to consider. Blind spots may exist, especially early on.

Love delights!

This was my favorite "reading" from all of the individuals who shared with me some of their most loving, passionate, vulnerable moments, because of the love they had for another human being. Love has made people do crazy things and the memories stay with us forever. Sharing your heart and soul with another and going beyond your limits with them makes you realize how much they mean to you. You would go to the end of the earth for them, as long as they stuck by your side. Some of the volunteers literally have done so.

So, here are the craziest things that the people I questioned have ever done for love. Some answers may surprise you, some are a bit odd, some romantic, some funny, some jaded, and some people have yet to do anything crazy for love, so they didn't make the list.

For Love:

Paul: "A nice goodbye and made crazy faces."

Rachel: "Sat through *The Lord of the Rings*: TWICE."

Vandre: "Quitting a job where I was making over $72,000 a year and I was only twenty-one-years old, I know it sounds totally stupid, but I don't regret it a bit, and moving from Brazil to the United States to be with the person I loved."

Eddie (35): "Flew to Europe to see if someone was right for me."

Bruno: "Stayed in an $800.00 a night hotel just to do something spontaneous… nice hotel, though!"

Lauren: "Moved to another country."

Jim: "Ask my lawyer. Being facetious. Is that a word?"

(Facetious: amusing, not to be taken seriously or literally.)

Jerry: "This is a tough one. I have done some crazy things. I once allowed a lady to be very selfish without using my good judgment to correct that. I eventually had to stop communicating with her for my own self-respect. I still love her."

Jessica: "Ran away from it."

Colleen: "I moved 1,500 miles for love. Was it worth it? No. Did I learn from it? Yes."

Lynn: "Made love on an abandoned train when I was drinking."

Carol: "Had sex with another woman while my partner watched. Craziest and stupidest thing ever. I feel that played a hand in our relationship having problems. Someone in this kind of 'game' always loses."

Gabriel: "I tried my damnedest to believe a lie, but obviously, that wasn't going to pan out in the end."

Ari (25): "I actually was once 'that girl on the side' in order to obtain a bond with the one who I thought shared a love for me. It eventually turned into a rude awakening. I was really bitter about it when it stopped, but over time, I learned a lesson and was able to find myself, without having to depend on a man. I guess I wouldn't regret being with that person, even when realizing how awful it was."

Donna: "I moved 1,000 miles to be near the guy I was seeing."

David: "I proposed to my ex-fiancée and spent money on a ring. Marriage makes absolutely no sense, nor does spending a ton of money on a ring, but when you're in love you do irrational things. Living together without marriage is that same thing without the 'paper.' All the paper does is makes it hard to get out of the relationship and adds a cost to the relationship if things head south. It makes absolutely no sense at all. Yet despite my rational, clear, judgment, I proposed to the girl I love. And boy do I love that girl!"

Another volunteer said he thought the craziest thing he had ever done for love was also "Bought a diamond ring."

Elizabeth: "Abandoned my family, friends, and goals to support someone else."

Mario hasn't done anything crazy for love, but I had to add his answer because it was so sweet and comical: "I don't know, I don't consider anything that I have done crazy, whatever I have done, I did it because I cared and because I wanted her to know I cared. I really don't think I have done anything crazy, I think skydiving is crazy. I haven't done that. Maybe I'm boring? Oh, crap."

Sonia (38, there were two different volunteers named Sonia): "Went away with an ex while he was involved in a new relationship."

Raul: "Proposing and taking the diamond ring off the wedding dress of a porcelain doll that I gave my fiancé for her birthday."

Ron (61): "Got married!!" Four other people had the same answer.

Mark: "Traveled many miles on weekends, spent many dollars on the phone trying to maintain a long-distance relationship."

Christi: "Stayed with a man for twenty-three years! Lost my youth all for the sake of the family unit and wanting to BELIEVE in love!"

Jessica: "Drove across the state every weekend to see him."

Here are some answers from volunteers who were anonymous:

"Lost a house and car to support my boyfriend who had PTSD from the war."

"Tried to change myself for my partner."

"Gave it my all when I should have known it was absolutely hopeless."

"Flew to Florida because he was lonely."

"Did whatever they wanted to do instead of what I wanted to do."

"Stalked someone." An example of love (or what they thought was love) gone terribly wrong.

"Acted like an idiot."

"Took a man to Italy as he was a poor school teacher. Paid all the expenses then found out he had a serious girlfriend, but really wanted to see Italy."

"Moved halfway across the country."

"Drove to another state just to say hi."

"Signed myself up for seven A.M shifts just to spend time with him."

"I drove and paid for everything for my ex-boyfriend and me for the first eight months of our relationship. He didn't have a job or car."

"Stopped my college studies."

"Travelled to the east coast while living on the west to see that person."

"Lied."

"Cared too much."

"Planned a backpacking trip to the Smokies before we knew each other's names."

"Bought a necklace when I hadn't even met her in person yet."

"Cheated."

"Used sex toys."

"Tried to be someone I'm not to try and impress the other person and be who they wanted me to be. Big mistake!"

"I once climbed in the back of a really small car so we could all ride together and I was feeling claustrophobic, but my needs did not matter, it only mattered that this was what he wanted. I was crazy, not anymore."

"Bought a house for the woman I loved. She moved in and I was going to move in with her later so we would be together. But six months after that she broke up with me instead and I ended up with a tenant."

"Told him that I would put him through law school."

"I don't remember, it has been more than thirty years." (I just had to include this one.)

And my favorite answer, again, was from Emiliya (she had some great answers!):

"Moved across the country, drove hours, called 100 times, stripped, danced, colored my hair brown, cried, ran, laughed, forgotten, and forgave."

As for me, you ask? I thought I was living a fairytale and followed my heart instead of my head, because I was crazy in love and believed.

Love involves compromise, as well as putting your partner's needs above your own at times. Most importantly: always respect yourself and cease giving up your soul in the bargain!

As you have seen, we all want to believe in something. It might be love, standing on your own two feet alone for the first time, opening the doors to your new business, getting the degree you've been striving to achieve, or simply obtaining more peace and happiness. One reason I love children so much is they don't possess many inhibitions. They live in the here and now and embrace each day. They tell it like it is because they don't know any better, and wear the love they have for you and desperately want in return on their sleeve.

In February 2012, Daniel O'Leary (Stony Brook University, N.Y.) and colleagues studied 274 married individuals in the U.S. who were married for ten years or more to determine how common long term-romantic love actually is. To the researchers' bewilderment, 46% of women and 49% of men reported being "very intensely in love." Physical affection, feeling positive about your partner (not taking them for granted but instead cherishing what they bring to the relationship), shared experiences, and individual personal happiness were all factors that contributed to positive views toward their marriage. I couldn't agree more.

When my friends want my opinion about something, I tell them my thoughts on the matter and often say, "Take from it what you wish and discard the rest." My answers are always backed with utmost care and concern. People need to make their own decisions to empower themselves. I don't want to give my clients all the answers. I want to assist them in becoming the best version of themselves so they can live a life filled with more passion and fulfillment, whatever that means to them. Although I don't know most of you personally, I really do care. I care about people and the betterment of the world in general. To become a better, drama-free dater is to whole-heartedly believe in yourself, since after all, are you not worth it? To see things as they are, to demand the respect you deserve, and to hold out for something truly remarkable. If you do this and follow some of the basics in this book and let go of trying to change the person you get involved with, or become strong enough to walk away from someone who is not treating you as you deserve because you're lonely, you'll eventually be happy you did. It <u>is</u> possible to create the love you have always dreamed of and to feel totally content in your relationship. It all starts and leads back to you and feeling good about yourself.

"Love yourself first and everything else falls into line."—Lucille Ball.

So, as the years go by, looks fade, and body parts don't work as well as they once did, find someone to share life with that you still look forward to talking to at the end of the day.

Enjoy each other, gaze into one another's eyes, hold hands, hang on your partner's every word, enjoy intimate moments, go to the beach on a rainy day, laugh until you cry, and follow your heart—it "will" lead the way.

So, dear readers, if you are fortunate enough to find someone you can not only live with, but surely can't live without, who is by your side, not only when things are wonderful, but when you are at your worst- down in the trenches, and their love radiates through your soul, then consider yourself lucky, know you are truly blessed, and never let them go.

References

1. "America's Families and Living Arrangements": 2011 United States Census Bureau.
2. Match.com and Chadwick Martin Bailey 2009–2010: "Studies on Recent Trends: Online Dating."
3. "Searching for a Mate: The Rise of the Internet as a Social Intermediary." Michael J. Rosenfeld, Stanford University and Reuben J. Thomas, The City College of New York. American Sociological Review 77 (4): 523–547.
4. "Instant Messages vs. Speech: Hormones and why we still need to hear each other." Leslie J. Seltzer, Ashley R. Prososki, Toni E. Ziegler and Seth D. Pollak. Evolution and Human Behavior, Volume 33, Issue 1, January 2012.
5. "Teens, Kindness and Cruelty on Social Network Sites: How American teens navigate the new world of 'digital citizenship'." Amanda Lenhart, Mary Madden, Aaron Smith, Kristen Purcell, Kathryn Zickuhr and Lee Rainie. Pew Research Project, November 11, 2011.
6. "Calling vs. Texting: Why Singles Text First Despite Their Preference to Call." http://www.itsjustlunchblog.com/2013.
7. http://en.wikipedia.org/wiki/First_date_(meeting).
8. Realisticats.blogspot.com/p/unrealistic_first_date_expectations.html.
9. "Why Men are settling for Mrs. Good Enough." Jessica Bennett reports. http://www.thedailybeast.com/articles/2012/02/21/why-men-are-settling-for-mrs-good-enough.html.

10. "The Stages of Committed Relationships," The Relationship Institute, Royal Oak, Michigan.
11. "How Much Should You Compromise for Your Relationship?" Psychology Today. Published on June 24, 2011 by Mark D. White, Ph.D. in "Maybe It's Just Me, But.."
12. *The 5 Love Languages. The Secret to Love That Lasts.* Gary Chapman. Northfield Publishing, Chicago, IL., 2010.
13. "Compatibility or Restraint? The Effects of Sexual Timing on Marriage Relationships." Dean M. Busby, Jason S. Carroll and Brian J. Willoughby. Journal of Family Psychology, 2010; 24 (6).
14. "How Delaying Intimacy Can Benefit Your Relationship." Brett & Kate McKay. The Art of Manliness, July 1, 2013.
15. "Neuroimaging of Love: FMRI Meta-Analysis Evidence toward New Perspectives in Sexual Medicine." Stephanie Ortigue, Francesco Bianchi-Demicheli, Nisa Patel, Chris Frum and James W. Lewis. The Journal of Sexual Medicine, 2010.
16. *The Triangle of Love: Intimacy, Passion, Commitment.* Robert J. Sternberg. Basic Books, Inc. New York, September, 1988.
17. "10 Elements of a Soul Mate?" Dr. Carmen Harra PH.D. Huffington Post, July 17, 2013.
18. Long-Term Love More Than a Rare Phenomenon? If So, What Are Its Correlates?" K. Daniel O'Leary, Bianca P. Acevedo, Arthur Aron, Leonie Huddy, and Debra Mashek. Social Psychological and Personality Science, August 5, 2011.
19. *The Art & Science of Love (DVD workshop).* The Gottman Institute, 2011. John Gottman, PH.D. and Julie Schwartz Gottman, PH.D.
20. "Suppression Sours Sacrifice: Emotional and Relational Costs of Suppressing Emotions in Romantic Relationships." Emily A. Impett, Aleksandr Kogan, Tammy English, Oliver John, Christopher Oveis, Amie M. Gordon, and Dacher Keltner. Personality and Social Psychology Bulletin 38 (6) 707–720, May 11, 2012.
21. "What Married Couples want from each other during Conflicts: An Investigation of Underlying Concerns". Sanford, Keith, and Kristin L. Wolfe. Journal of Social and Clinical Psychology 32.6 (2013): 674–699.

22. "Love of Their Life? 1 in 7 People Don't Think Their Partner Is, 46 Percent Would Leave Current Partner If Their 'True Love' Came Around." HNGN, August 2013.
23. "Americans Can't Put Down Their Smartphones, Even During Sex." Jumio.com, July 11, 2013.
24. "Benefit or Burden? Attraction in Cross-Sex Friendship." Journal of Social and Personal Relationships August 2012, Vol. 29, No. 5, 569–596.
25. U.S. Census Bureau/Census.gov. Income, Poverty and Health Insurance Coverage in the United States: 2012. Tuesday, September 17, 2013.
26. "Sexual Regret: Evidence for Evolved Sex Differences." Andrew Galperin, Martie G. Haselton, David A. Frederick, Joshua Poore, William von Hippel, David M. Buss, Gian C. Gonzaga. Archives of Sexual Behavior, October 2013, Volume 42, Issue 7, pp 1145–1161.
27. www.phrases.org.uk/meanings.
28. Evolution and Human Behavior Volume 36, Issue 1, January 2015, Pages 73–79.
29. Francis, Andrew M. and Mialon, Hugo M., 'A Diamond is Forever' and Other Fairy Tales: The Relationship between Wedding Expenses and Marriage Duration (September 15, 2014).
30. https://www.phactual.com/16-scary-statistics-of-online-dating/.
31. http://crimefeed.com/2016/03/match-made-in-hell-five-online-dates-ending-in-murder/.
32. https://docs.justia.com/cases/federal/districtcourts/nevada/nvdce/2:2013cv00097/92214/18.
33. "What to Know About Tinder in 5 Charts." Written by Felim McGrath. (www.globalwebindex.net/blog/aothor/felim-mcgrath) on Friday, April 24, 2015.
34. Pew Research Center: "5 Facts about Online Dating," by Aaron Smith (http://www.pewresearch.org/staffaaron-smith/) and Monica Anderson. (http://www.pewresearch.org/author/manderson/).
35. Paul Aditi. Cyberpsychology, Behavior, and Social Networking. October 2014, 17 (10): 664–667. doi:10.1089/cyber.2014.0302.

About the Author

Camie Vincent is a psychotherapist licensed in Georgia and Florida, currently working in private practice in the Atlanta, GA. area. She is a member of Psi Chi- The International Honor Society In Psychology and is listed under the National Crime Victims Research & Treatment Center of South Carolina. A world traveler who appreciates the little things in life, she writes an advice column for dating/relationships, is a romantic at heart, and wholeheartedly believes in love. Visit her at http://asteptowardchange.com and http://dearladylove.com.

CPSIA information can be obtained
at www.ICGtesting.com
Printed in the USA
BVHW03s0650200518
516773BV00015B/466/P